My First Steps in the Stock Market:
A Beginner's Guide to Building Wealth Through Smart Investing

PUBLISHED BY Gavin Mercer

Table of contents

Introduction: The Individual Investor's Advantage

The financial landscape has fundamentally shifted in favor of individual investors in ways that would have seemed impossible just two decades ago. Commission-free trading, institutional-quality research tools, and access to global markets that once required millions of dollars in assets are now available to anyone with a smartphone and a few hundred dollars to invest. Yet despite these unprecedented advantages, studies consistently show that the average individual investor significantly underperforms even basic market indices, often by margins that compound into hundreds of thousands or millions of dollars in lost wealth over investing lifetimes.

This performance gap doesn't stem from lack of intelligence, insufficient information, or limited market access. Instead, it reflects a fundamental misunderstanding of what successful investing actually requires and how to harness the unique advantages that individual investors possess over their institutional counterparts. While Wall Street professionals struggle with quarterly performance pressures, regulatory constraints, and redemption risks that force suboptimal timing decisions, individual investors can maintain positions through complete market cycles, concentrate in their highest-conviction ideas, and implement long-term strategies that institutional investors simply cannot pursue effectively.

The irony of modern investing lies in this contradiction: individual investors have never had better tools or greater opportunities, yet they continue to achieve inferior results through behavioral mistakes, strategic errors, and misguided attempts to replicate institutional approaches that ignore their natural advantages. The solution isn't more complex strategies or exotic investments, but rather a systematic understanding of how markets actually work, why individual investors consistently make predictable mistakes, and how to construct investment approaches that align with both market realities and human psychology.

Consider the story of Sarah Chen, a software engineer who began investing in 2015 with no formal financial education beyond a basic understanding of retirement account contributions. Like most beginning investors, she started by purchasing individual stocks based on news articles and analyst recommendations, trading frequently as her confidence grew with early gains during the bull market. By 2018, despite a strong overall market performance, her portfolio lagged the S&P 500 by more than eight percentage points annually due to poor timing, excessive trading costs, and emotional decisions that led her to buy high and sell low repeatedly.

The wake-up call came during the March 2020 market decline when fear drove her to sell her entire portfolio near the market bottom, crystallizing significant losses just weeks before one of the strongest market recoveries in history. This painful experience forced her to acknowledge that her approach was fundamentally flawed and that success would require developing genuine expertise rather than relying on intuition and market timing attempts.

Over the following months, Sarah committed herself to systematic education about investment principles, market history, and behavioral psychology. She learned about the power of compound returns, the impossibility of consistent market timing, and the psychological biases that had undermined her decision-making. More importantly, she developed an investment philosophy based on long-term business ownership, systematic diversification, and emotional discipline that enabled her to ignore short-term market noise while focusing on wealth building over decades rather than quarters.

By 2024, Sarah's transformed approach had generated returns that exceeded market averages while requiring far less time and emotional energy than her previous trading-focused strategy. Her success didn't come from superior stock selection or market timing abilities, but from understanding fundamental principles and implementing them consistently while avoiding the behavioral traps that continue to ensnare most individual investors.

Sarah's transformation illustrates the central thesis of this comprehensive guide: successful investing is primarily about avoiding mistakes rather than finding exceptional opportunities, and individual investors possess inherent advantages that can generate superior long-term returns when properly understood and systematically exploited. The key lies not in competing with institutions on their terms, but in leveraging the unique advantages that come with patient capital, flexible time horizons, and freedom from the constraints that limit institutional performance.

The democratization of investment tools and information has created an unprecedented opportunity for individual investors to achieve institutional-quality portfolio management while maintaining the strategic flexibility that large institutions cannot match. Exchange-traded funds provide instant diversification across any asset class or geographic region at costs that would have been impossible for individual investors to achieve through direct investment just twenty years ago. Robo-advisors offer sophisticated portfolio optimization and tax management services that rival those provided by private wealth managers to ultra-high-net-worth families. Alternative data sources provide insights into economic trends and business performance that were previously available only to professional analysts with substantial research budgets.

Yet these technological advantages remain largely unrealized by most individual investors who continue to focus on stock picking, market timing, and short-term performance rather than developing the systematic approaches and long-term perspectives that create lasting wealth. The proliferation of investment options and analytical tools has paradoxically made investing more challenging for many individuals who become overwhelmed by choices and complexity rather than empowered by expanded capabilities.

This guide addresses that challenge by providing a structured framework for understanding investment fundamentals while building practical skills that can be applied immediately and refined over decades of market participation. Rather than focusing on specific investment recommendations that become obsolete as market conditions change, we concentrate on timeless principles and analytical frameworks that remain relevant regardless of economic cycles, technological developments, or regulatory changes.

The journey begins with understanding the psychological foundations of investment success, as behavioral factors represent the primary determinant of long-term investment outcomes. Academic research consistently shows that investor behavior explains more performance variation than asset allocation, security selection, or market timing combined, yet most investment education ignores psychology in favor of technical analysis that proves largely irrelevant for long-term wealth building.

We then progress through the fundamental skills necessary for intelligent investment analysis, including financial statement interpretation, valuation methodologies, and risk assessment techniques that enable informed decision-making without requiring professional-level expertise or excessive time commitments. These analytical tools provide the foundation for independent investment evaluation while helping you avoid common pitfalls that trap investors who rely solely on external recommendations or popular market trends.

Portfolio construction and risk management receive extensive attention as these strategic decisions ultimately determine investment outcomes far more than individual security selection. Understanding how different asset classes behave during various market conditions enables sophisticated diversification strategies that can reduce risk while maintaining growth potential through approaches that most individual investors never consider.

The exploration extends beyond traditional domestic investing to encompass international opportunities, alternative investment strategies, and emerging technologies that are reshaping the investment landscape while creating new opportunities for individual investors willing to develop appropriate expertise. These advanced topics provide natural progression paths for investors who master fundamental concepts while seeking additional diversification or return enhancement opportunities.

Throughout this comprehensive exploration, we maintain focus on practical implementation rather than theoretical perfection, recognizing that successful investing requires balancing optimal strategies with realistic capabilities and constraints that characterize most individual investors' situations. The goal is not to transform you into a professional money manager, but to provide the knowledge and tools necessary to make informed decisions while avoiding the costly mistakes that undermine most individual investors' wealth-building efforts.

The integration of these various components creates a comprehensive framework for investment success that can adapt to changing market conditions while maintaining consistency with fundamental principles that govern long-term wealth creation. This framework recognizes that different investors possess different capabilities, constraints, and objectives while providing flexible approaches that can be customized based on individual circumstances and preferences.

The ultimate objective extends beyond simple portfolio management to encompass the creation of lasting wealth that provides financial security, opportunity, and potential legacy for future generations. This wealth-building process requires patience, discipline, and strategic thinking that extends beyond short-term market movements to focus on the compound growth that creates extraordinary outcomes over multiple decades.

The timing for this comprehensive approach to individual investing has never been better, as current market conditions provide both opportunities and challenges that reward sophisticated analysis while punishing speculative behavior and short-term thinking. Economic uncertainty, technological disruption, and demographic changes are creating investment opportunities that favor patient, well-informed investors while challenging those who lack systematic approaches or long-term perspectives.

The pages that follow represent more than an investment education; they constitute a roadmap for financial empowerment that can transform your relationship with money while providing the knowledge and confidence necessary to navigate any market environment. The concepts and strategies presented here have been tested through multiple market cycles and proven effective for investors willing to commit to continuous learning and disciplined execution.

Your success will not depend on predicting market movements, identifying the next hot stock, or timing economic cycles.

Instead, it will reflect your ability to understand fundamental principles, maintain emotional discipline, and implement systematic approaches that harness the natural advantages available to patient, well-informed individual investors.

The journey begins with a single decision to take control of your financial future through education, discipline, and systematic action. The knowledge gained through this comprehensive exploration will serve you for decades while potentially creating wealth that transforms not only your own life but the lives of those you care about most. The markets are waiting, the tools are available, and the opportunity is unprecedented. Your investment education starts now.

Chapter 1: The Psychology of Successful Investing

1.1 Understanding the Investor's Mind

The human brain, evolved over millions of years to help our ancestors survive in hostile environments, carries within it a complex array of cognitive biases and emotional responses that served us well when facing immediate physical threats. Yet these same mental mechanisms that once helped humans avoid predators and secure food now create systematic obstacles to investment success in modern financial markets.

When Sarah Mitchell first opened her brokerage account in 2019, she believed that successful investing was primarily about analyzing company fundamentals, reading financial statements, and following market trends. Like many new investors, she assumed that intelligence and research would naturally translate into profitable decisions. What she discovered over the following months was far more humbling: despite her MBA in finance and years of experience as a corporate analyst, her investment returns consistently lagged the market indices she thought she could easily outperform.

Sarah's experience reflects a fundamental truth about investing that most people discover only through painful experience. The greatest obstacle to investment success is not a lack of information, insufficient analytical tools, or inadequate market access. Instead, the primary barrier exists within the three pounds of neural tissue between our ears. The human brain, remarkable as it is, comes equipped with cognitive and emotional patterns that systematically interfere with the rational decision-making that successful investing requires.

Consider the evolutionary context that shaped our mental architecture. For hundreds of thousands of years, human survival depended on making rapid decisions with incomplete information. Those who hesitated when faced with potential danger rarely lived long enough to pass on their genes. Those who overreacted to false alarms lived to reproduce another day. This survival-oriented programming created mental shortcuts—what psychologists call heuristics—that prioritize speed over accuracy and emotional safety over analytical precision.

In the investment world, these ancient survival mechanisms manifest as predictable behavioral patterns that consistently undermine portfolio performance. The same mental processes that once helped humans navigate physical dangers now cause investors to buy high during market euphoria and sell low during periods of panic. The brain's tendency to seek patterns in random data leads investors to chase hot investment trends that have already run their course. The evolutionary preference for immediate gratification over delayed rewards causes investors to focus on short-term price movements rather than long-term value creation.

The field of behavioral finance, pioneered by researchers like Daniel Kahneman and Amos Tversky, has systematically documented these psychological obstacles to rational investing. Their work revealed that humans are not the rational economic actors that traditional financial theory assumed. Instead, we are predictably irrational in ways that create consistent patterns of suboptimal investment behavior.

Loss aversion represents perhaps the most significant psychological barrier to investment success. Research consistently shows that the pain of losing money feels roughly twice as intense as the pleasure of gaining the same amount. This asymmetric emotional response to gains and losses creates a powerful bias toward avoiding potential losses, even when the probability of gain significantly exceeds the risk of loss. In practice, loss aversion manifests as excessive conservatism in investment selection, reluctance to realize losses even when rational analysis suggests cutting losses, and a tendency to hold losing investments too long while selling winners too quickly.

The endowment effect compounds this challenge by causing investors to value investments they already own more highly than identical investments they do not own. Once we purchase a stock, bond, or fund, psychological ownership creates an emotional attachment that clouds objective evaluation. This attachment makes it difficult to sell investments that are no longer attractive simply because we own them. The combination of loss aversion and the endowment effect creates a powerful psychological force that keeps investors trapped in deteriorating positions.

Confirmation bias represents another crucial psychological obstacle that prevents investors from making rational decisions. This tendency to seek, interpret, and remember information in ways that confirm our existing beliefs means that once we form an opinion about an investment, we unconsciously filter subsequent information to support that view while dismissing contradictory evidence. An investor who purchases shares in a technology company will tend to notice and remember positive news about the company while downplaying or ignoring negative developments. This selective attention to confirming evidence prevents the objective reassessment that successful investing requires.

The availability heuristic causes investors to overweight recent or memorable events when making decisions. Because dramatic market crashes receive extensive media coverage and create lasting emotional memories, many investors overestimate the likelihood of catastrophic losses. Conversely, during bull markets, the recent memory of rising prices makes continued gains seem more probable than historical data would suggest. This mental shortcut causes investors to extrapolate recent trends into the future, leading to poor timing decisions that consistently buy into euphoria and sell into despair.

Herding behavior emerges from deep evolutionary roots that once provided safety in numbers. In the investment context, this manifests as a tendency to follow the crowd rather than maintain independent judgment. When friends, colleagues, and media commentators all express enthusiasm for a particular investment theme, the social pressure to conform can override rational analysis. The dot-com bubble of the late 1990s and the housing bubble of the mid-2000s both demonstrated how powerful herding instincts can drive entire markets away from fundamental values.

Overconfidence bias leads many investors to overestimate their ability to predict market movements and select winning investments. This excessive confidence in one's own judgment results in insufficient diversification, excessive trading, and inadequate risk management. Studies consistently show that the most confident investors tend to achieve the lowest returns, primarily because their confidence leads them to make more frequent trades that generate transaction costs without adding value.

The planning fallacy causes investors to underestimate the time, costs, and risks involved in achieving their investment goals while overestimating the benefits. This optimistic bias leads to unrealistic expectations about investment returns and inadequate preparation for periods of poor performance. When reality fails to match these optimistic projections, investors often abandon sound long-term strategies in favor of more speculative approaches that promise quicker results.

Mental accounting creates artificial divisions between different pools of money that should be evaluated as part of a comprehensive financial picture. Investors might maintain a conservative approach in their retirement accounts while speculating aggressively with money designated for other purposes, failing to recognize that their overall financial risk profile depends on their total investment exposure. This compartmentalized thinking prevents optimal asset allocation and can lead to contradictory investment strategies across different accounts.

Anchoring bias causes investors to rely too heavily on the first piece of information they receive about an investment. If an investor first learns about a stock when it's trading at $100 per share, that price becomes an anchor that influences all subsequent valuation judgments. Even when the company's fundamentals deteriorate significantly, the investor may continue to view $80 as "cheap" relative to the original $100 anchor, despite the possibility that the stock's intrinsic value has fallen to $60.

The sunk cost fallacy leads investors to continue funding losing investments simply because they have already invested money in them. Rather than evaluating whether additional investment makes sense based on future prospects, investors often throw good money after bad in an attempt to justify previous decisions. This emotional attachment to past investments prevents the objective evaluation necessary for optimal portfolio management.

Understanding these psychological obstacles represents the first step toward overcoming them. Successful investors develop systems and processes designed to counteract their natural biases rather than relying on willpower or intelligence alone. They recognize that the human brain, magnificent as it is, requires external support systems to function effectively in the complex and counterintuitive world of financial markets.

The path to investment success begins with honest self-assessment and humble recognition of our psychological limitations. Only by acknowledging these built-in biases can investors begin to develop the mental frameworks and behavioral practices that lead to better long-term outcomes. The following sections will explore specific strategies for overcoming these psychological obstacles and building the mental discipline that successful investing requires.

1.2 Building Your Investor Mindset

The transformation from emotional, reactive decision-making to disciplined, systematic investing requires more than intellectual understanding of psychological biases. It demands a fundamental shift in how we think about money, risk, and our role in the financial markets. Building the proper investor mindset involves developing new mental habits, reframing our relationship with uncertainty, and cultivating the patience that long-term wealth creation requires.

The foundation of a successful investor mindset begins with accepting uncertainty as a permanent feature of investing rather than a temporary obstacle to overcome. Most people approach investing with the unconscious expectation that enough research, analysis, or expert advice will eventually eliminate uncertainty and guarantee positive outcomes. This expectation sets investors up for frustration and poor decisions when markets inevitably behave in unpredictable ways.

Consider the story of David Chen, a software engineer who spent two years developing an elaborate spreadsheet model to predict stock movements. His model incorporated dozens of financial metrics, technical indicators, and macroeconomic variables. Despite the sophistication of his approach, David's investment results remained disappointing because he focused on trying to eliminate uncertainty rather than learning to make good decisions despite uncertainty. Only when David shifted his focus from prediction to preparation did his investment performance begin to improve.

The mature investor mindset embraces uncertainty as the source of investment returns rather than an enemy to defeat. Markets compensate investors precisely because outcomes are uncertain. If future stock prices were predictable, there would be no reason for markets to offer positive expected returns. This fundamental insight transforms uncertainty from a source of anxiety into an accepted reality that makes investing possible.

Developing comfort with uncertainty requires practice and deliberate mental conditioning. Successful investors learn to distinguish between what they can control and what they cannot. They focus their energy on controllable factors like asset allocation, diversification, costs, and investment time horizon while accepting that short-term market movements, economic cycles, and geopolitical events remain largely outside their influence.

The concept of probabilistic thinking represents another crucial component of the investor mindset. Rather than thinking in terms of certainties, successful investors think in terms of probabilities and expected values. They understand that any individual investment decision might turn out poorly despite being analytically sound, while a series of good decisions will likely produce favorable outcomes over time.

This probabilistic framework helps investors maintain emotional equilibrium during periods of poor performance. When a well-researched investment declines in value, the probabilistic thinker recognizes that negative outcomes are part of the expected range of possibilities rather than evidence of analytical failure. This perspective prevents the emotional spiral that often leads investors to abandon sound strategies during temporary setbacks.

Building an effective investor mindset also requires developing a personal investment philosophy that serves as an anchor during turbulent periods. This philosophy should reflect your values, risk tolerance, and long-term objectives while providing clear guidelines for decision-making when emotions run high. The specific content of the philosophy matters less than having a coherent framework that can guide decisions consistently over time.

Some investors adopt a value-oriented philosophy focused on purchasing high-quality businesses at reasonable prices and holding them for extended periods. Others embrace growth investing, seeking companies with exceptional prospects for expansion. Still others prefer a more quantitative approach, using systematic strategies based on historical patterns in market data. The key is choosing an approach that aligns with your temperament and sticking with it through various market conditions.

The process of developing this philosophy requires honest self-assessment about your risk tolerance, time horizon, and emotional reactions to volatility. Many investors discover significant gaps between their stated risk tolerance and their actual behavior during market stress. Building a sustainable investor mindset means calibrating your approach to match your true emotional capacity rather than your idealized self-image.

Patience emerges as perhaps the most valuable trait in the investor's mental toolkit. The power of compound returns requires time to manifest, but the modern world provides constant pressure for immediate results. Social media, financial news, and portfolio tracking applications create an environment where investors can monitor their performance minute by minute, fostering short-term thinking that undermines long-term success.

Cultivating patience requires deliberately limiting exposure to short-term performance information while focusing attention on longer-term progress indicators. This might involve checking portfolio values monthly rather than daily, concentrating on annual rather than quarterly performance, and measuring success in terms of progress toward long-term goals rather than comparison to recent market movements.

The investor mindset also involves developing what psychologists call a growth mindset rather than a fixed mindset about investing capabilities. Investors with a fixed mindset believe their investment skills are largely predetermined and unchangeable. When they experience losses or poor performance, they interpret these outcomes as evidence of their inherent limitations. This interpretation often leads to giving up on active investment management in favor of completely passive approaches or abandoning investing altogether.

In contrast, investors with a growth mindset view setbacks as learning opportunities and believe their skills can improve through study, practice, and reflection. They analyze both successful and unsuccessful decisions to extract lessons that inform future choices. This learning orientation helps them continuously refine their approach while maintaining confidence in their ability to improve over time.

Building the proper investor mindset requires conscious effort to counteract the natural human tendency toward overconfidence following periods of good performance and excessive pessimism during downturns. Successful investors develop emotional stability by maintaining perspective during both winning and losing streaks, recognizing that short-term results often reflect luck as much as skill.

Chapter 2: Decoding the Market Ecosystem

The New York Stock Exchange processes over 1.5 billion shares daily, yet seventy percent of all trading is now executed by algorithms operating at speeds measured in microseconds. This transformation of financial markets from human-dominated trading floors to computer-driven networks represents one of the most significant structural changes in modern finance. Understanding this complex ecosystem is crucial for individual investors to find their edge and navigate markets that have evolved far beyond the simple buyer-seller dynamics that most people imagine.

2.1 The Players and Their Motivations

Modern financial markets operate as a vast, interconnected ecosystem where different types of participants pursue varied objectives with dramatically different resources, time horizons, and constraints. The interactions between these diverse market participants create the complex dynamics that drive daily price movements, long-term trends, and periodic episodes of extreme volatility that can confound even experienced investors.

Institutional vs. retail dynamics: How pension funds, hedge funds, and individual investors create market movements

The most fundamental distinction in modern markets exists between institutional and retail investors, two groups that operate with vastly different capabilities, motivations, and constraints. Institutional investors control the vast majority of investment capital and trading volume, yet their behavior patterns create opportunities and challenges that individual investors must understand to succeed.

Pension funds represent perhaps the most important category of institutional investor, managing trillions of dollars in retirement assets for millions of workers. These massive pools of capital operate under unique constraints that create predictable behavior patterns. Pension funds have extremely long investment horizons, often measured in decades, and face regulatory requirements to match their assets with future pension obligations. This creates a natural preference for stable, dividend-paying stocks and long-term bonds that can provide predictable income streams.

The sheer size of pension fund assets means that their investment decisions can move entire markets. When the California Public Employees' Retirement System, known as CalPERS, decides to increase its allocation to international stocks, the resulting capital flows can influence currency markets and boost stock prices in targeted countries. Individual investors who understand these institutional flow patterns can position themselves to benefit from the resulting price movements.

Pension funds also face unique timing pressures that create opportunities for more nimble investors. As baby boomers retire in increasing numbers, many pension systems must sell assets to fund current benefit payments. This demographic shift creates predictable selling pressure in certain asset classes, particularly long-term bonds and dividend-focused equity strategies that have been popular with pension managers.

Endowments and foundations represent another crucial category of institutional investor with distinct characteristics that influence market behavior. University endowments like those managed by Harvard and Yale have pioneered alternative investment strategies that emphasize private equity, hedge funds, and real estate over traditional stock and bond portfolios. Their success with these approaches has influenced other institutional investors to pursue similar strategies, creating significant capital flows into alternative asset classes.

The endowment model typically involves high allocations to illiquid investments that cannot be easily sold during market stress. This illiquidity can force endowments to sell their most liquid holdings during financial crises, creating temporary price distortions in public markets. The 2008 financial crisis demonstrated this dynamic when many endowments were forced to sell publicly traded stocks at depressed prices to meet cash flow needs while their private equity and real estate holdings remained frozen.

Hedge funds operate with fundamentally different objectives and constraints than pension funds or endowments. These investment vehicles typically charge high fees in exchange for pursuing absolute returns rather than simply matching market benchmarks. This fee structure creates powerful incentives for hedge fund managers to generate short-term performance that can attract additional investor capital.

The pursuit of absolute returns leads hedge funds to employ sophisticated strategies that can create significant market volatility. Quantitative hedge funds use complex mathematical models to identify tiny price discrepancies between related securities, then deploy massive amounts of leverage to profit from these inefficiencies. When these models signal similar opportunities simultaneously, the resulting trading activity can overwhelm normal market-making capacity and create dramatic price swings.

Event-driven hedge funds focus on profiting from corporate transactions like mergers, bankruptcies, and spin-offs. Their trading activity around these events can create unusual price patterns that affect individual investors. When a merger is announced, arbitrage funds typically purchase the target company's stock while shorting the acquirer's shares. This activity can drive the target's stock price close to the proposed acquisition price while creating selling pressure on the acquirer's shares.

Long-short equity hedge funds simultaneously hold long positions in stocks they believe are undervalued and short positions in stocks they consider overvalued. During market stress, these funds often face redemption pressure from investors seeking to withdraw capital. The resulting forced selling can exacerbate market declines as funds liquidate their most liquid positions to meet redemption requests.

Mutual funds and exchange-traded funds serve as intermediaries between institutional and retail investors, but their operational structures create unique dynamics that influence market behavior. Traditional mutual funds face daily redemption requests from individual investors, forcing fund managers to maintain cash reserves and potentially sell holdings during periods of high redemption activity. This dynamic can amplify market declines when fearful investors rush to redeem fund shares.

Exchange-traded funds have revolutionized investing by allowing individual investors to access sophisticated strategies and asset classes previously available only to institutions. However, the creation and redemption mechanism that keeps ETF prices aligned with their underlying assets can create temporary price distortions during periods of market stress. When ETF supply and demand becomes imbalanced, authorized participants must trade the underlying securities to restore equilibrium, potentially amplifying volatility in the underlying markets.

Index funds, whether structured as mutual funds or ETFs, have grown to represent a dominant force in equity markets. The passive nature of index investing means that capital flows into these funds translate directly into purchases of underlying stocks in proportion to their index weights. This mechanical buying can drive up prices of large-cap stocks that dominate major indices while providing less support for smaller companies with minimal index representation.

Individual retail investors, despite controlling a minority of total market capitalization, can significantly influence market dynamics during periods of extreme sentiment. The meme stock phenomenon of 2021 demonstrated how coordinated retail investor activity, amplified by social media and commission-free trading platforms, could drive dramatic price movements in specific securities. These episodes revealed that retail investors, when acting collectively, could temporarily overwhelm the normal price discovery mechanisms that institutional investors rely upon.

Retail investor behavior patterns differ significantly from institutional approaches in ways that create both opportunities and risks. Individual investors tend to be more influenced by recent performance, leading to momentum-driven buying during bull markets and panic selling during downturns. This pro-cyclical behavior often results in retail investors buying high and selling low, creating opportunities for more disciplined institutional investors to profit from these predictable patterns.

Market makers and liquidity providers: The hidden forces that keep markets functioning

Behind the visible drama of buying and selling decisions lies a complex infrastructure of market makers and liquidity providers who ensure that investors can trade securities efficiently without causing dramatic price impacts. These intermediaries operate largely invisibly to most investors, yet their activities fundamentally shape the trading environment and influence the costs and risks of portfolio management.

Traditional market makers operate by continuously quoting both bid and ask prices for specific securities, earning profits from the spread between these prices while providing liquidity to other market participants. This business model requires sophisticated risk management systems because market makers must hold inventory positions that expose them to price fluctuations while they search for offsetting trades.

The market-making business has evolved dramatically with the introduction of electronic trading systems and algorithmic decision-making. Modern market makers use complex algorithms to adjust their bid and ask prices continuously based on order flow patterns, inventory levels, and market volatility. These systems can process thousands of pricing decisions per second, enabling market makers to provide liquidity more efficiently while managing risk more precisely.

High-frequency trading firms represent the most advanced evolution of market-making technology. These organizations invest hundreds of millions of dollars in cutting-edge computer systems, specialized data connections, and proximity to exchange servers to gain microsecond advantages in processing market information. Their algorithms can detect and respond to price movements faster than traditional market participants, allowing them to provide liquidity while minimizing inventory risk.

The presence of sophisticated market makers generally benefits individual investors by reducing bid-ask spreads and ensuring that large orders can be executed without causing significant price impact. However, these benefits come with subtle costs that may not be immediately apparent to casual observers. Market makers must be compensated for the risks they assume, and this compensation ultimately comes from the investors who demand liquidity services.

During periods of extreme market stress, the limitations of modern market-making systems can become apparent. Algorithmic market makers typically reduce their activity or widen their bid-ask spreads when volatility increases beyond their risk management parameters. This defensive behavior can exacerbate market declines by reducing liquidity precisely when investors most need it.

The flash crash of May 6, 2010, demonstrated how quickly liquidity can evaporate when market-making algorithms encounter conditions outside their normal operating parameters. Within minutes, major stock indices declined by nearly ten percent before recovering most of their losses, highlighting the potential fragility of markets that depend heavily on algorithmic liquidity provision.

The role of algorithmic trading: How high-frequency trading affects your investments

Algorithmic trading now dominates financial markets to an extent that would have been unimaginable just two decades ago. These computer-driven systems execute trades based on predetermined rules and mathematical models, operating at speeds and scales that human traders cannot match. Understanding how these algorithms function and interact provides crucial insight into modern market dynamics.

High-frequency trading represents the most visible and controversial form of algorithmic trading. These systems attempt to profit from tiny price discrepancies that exist for only milliseconds, using extreme speed and sophisticated technology to capture profits that would be impossible for human traders to achieve. High-frequency trading firms compete intensely on execution speed, investing heavily in faster computers, more efficient algorithms, and closer physical proximity to exchange servers.

The impact of high-frequency trading on individual investors remains a subject of ongoing debate among market participants and regulators. Proponents argue that these systems improve market efficiency by quickly eliminating price discrepancies and providing continuous liquidity that reduces transaction costs for all market participants. Critics contend that high-frequency trading creates an unfair advantage for technologically sophisticated firms while potentially increasing market instability.

Empirical evidence suggests that high-frequency trading generally reduces bid-ask spreads and increases the amount of trading volume that markets can absorb without significant price impact. These improvements benefit individual investors by reducing the costs of buying and selling securities. However, the benefits may be offset by increased short-term volatility as algorithmic systems react rapidly to news and market movements.

Momentum algorithms represent another important category of algorithmic trading that can significantly influence short-term price movements. These systems attempt to identify and profit from trending price movements by buying securities that are rising and selling those that are declining. When multiple momentum algorithms identify the same trends simultaneously, their coordinated buying or selling activity can amplify price movements and create self-reinforcing cycles.

Mean reversion algorithms pursue the opposite strategy, attempting to profit from the tendency of prices to return toward their historical averages after periods of extreme movement. These systems typically buy securities that have declined significantly and sell those that have risen dramatically, providing a stabilizing influence that counteracts momentum-driven volatility.

The interaction between different algorithmic strategies creates complex feedback loops that can produce unexpected market behavior. During normal conditions, momentum and mean reversion algorithms often offset each other's activities, contributing to relatively stable price discovery. However, when external events cause one strategy type to dominate, the resulting algorithmic amplification can create dramatic price swings that seem disconnected from fundamental news.

Cross-market arbitrage algorithms continuously monitor price relationships between related securities and markets, executing trades when these relationships deviate from their normal patterns. These systems help maintain efficient pricing across different exchanges and asset classes, but their activity can also transmit volatility rapidly across global markets.

Statistical arbitrage represents a sophisticated form of algorithmic trading that attempts to profit from temporary price relationships between large portfolios of securities. These systems use complex mathematical models to identify stocks that appear temporarily mispriced relative to their historical relationships with other securities. The resulting trading activity can influence individual stock prices in ways that may seem disconnected from company-specific news or fundamentals.

For individual investors, understanding algorithmic trading patterns provides valuable context for interpreting short-term price movements and market behavior. Recognizing that much of the daily trading activity reflects algorithmic responses to technical patterns rather than fundamental analysis can help individual investors maintain perspective during periods of seemingly irrational market behavior.

The dominance of algorithmic trading also creates opportunities for patient, fundamentally-oriented investors who can look beyond short-term price noise to focus on underlying business values. While algorithms excel at processing large amounts of information quickly and identifying short-term patterns, they typically cannot replicate the kind of long-term, business-focused analysis that characterizes successful value investing approaches.

2.2 Market Mechanics Unveiled

Understanding how markets actually function beneath the surface reveals a complex mechanical infrastructure that most individual investors never see or consider. The process of converting an investment decision into an executed trade involves multiple intermediaries, sophisticated technological systems, and intricate regulatory frameworks that have evolved over decades to handle the enormous volume and complexity of modern financial markets.

When an individual investor clicks "buy" on their brokerage platform, that simple action triggers a complex sequence of events that occurs largely invisibly within milliseconds. The order first travels from the investor's device through their broker's systems, where it undergoes initial validation and risk checking. The broker must verify that the investor has sufficient funds for the purchase and that the order complies with various regulatory requirements before routing it to the appropriate trading venue.

The choice of where to send the order represents a crucial decision that can significantly impact the execution quality the investor receives. Unlike the popular image of a single stock exchange where all trading occurs, modern markets fragment across dozens of competing venues, each with different characteristics, fee structures, and participant bases. The broker must navigate this complex landscape to find the best available price for their customer's order.

Most retail orders flow through a process called payment for order flow, where brokers receive compensation from market makers in exchange for directing orders to specific trading venues. This arrangement allows brokers to offer commission-free trading to their customers while generating revenue from the market makers who value the predictable flow of retail orders. However, this system creates potential conflicts of interest between brokers and their customers, as brokers may prioritize the venues that pay them the most rather than those that provide the best execution quality.

Market makers who receive retail order flow typically provide price improvement over the publicly quoted bid and ask prices, meaning that investors often receive better execution than they would on traditional exchanges. This price improvement occurs because retail orders tend to be less informed than institutional orders, allowing market makers to offer more favorable pricing while still maintaining profitable spreads.

The concept of order types reveals another layer of complexity in market mechanics that can significantly impact execution outcomes. Market orders, which execute immediately at the best available price, provide certainty of execution but offer no price protection if market conditions change between order submission and execution. Limit orders specify the maximum price an investor is willing to pay or minimum price they will accept, providing price protection at the cost of execution uncertainty.

More sophisticated order types allow investors to implement complex trading strategies that would be impossible to execute manually. Stop-loss orders automatically convert to market orders when a security reaches a specified price, allowing investors to limit potential losses without constantly monitoring their positions. Stop-limit orders provide additional price protection by converting to limit orders rather than market orders when triggered, though this protection comes with increased risk that the order may not execute if the market moves rapidly.

Iceberg orders allow large institutional investors to hide the true size of their trading intentions by revealing only small portions of their total orders to the market at any given time. This prevents other market participants from front-running large orders or adjusting their own strategies based on knowledge of pending institutional activity.

The timing of order execution within market hours can significantly impact the prices investors receive due to predictable patterns in trading volume and volatility. The market opening period, known as the opening auction, typically experiences higher volatility as overnight news and information gets incorporated into prices through concentrated trading activity. Many professional traders avoid placing market orders during this period due to the increased risk of unfavorable execution.

The final hour of trading often sees increased volume as institutional investors adjust positions before market close and index funds execute trades related to benchmark rebalancing. This elevated activity can create opportunities for patient investors willing to time their trades carefully, though it also increases the risk of execution at unfavorable prices for those who must trade during these periods.

After-hours trading sessions extend market access beyond traditional trading hours but operate with significantly different characteristics than regular market sessions. Lower trading volumes during these periods can lead to wider bid-ask spreads and increased price volatility, particularly in response to earnings announcements or other significant news events that occur outside regular market hours.

The rise of dark pools represents one of the most significant structural changes in modern market mechanics. These private trading venues allow institutional investors to buy and sell large quantities of securities without revealing their intentions to the broader market. Dark pools reduce the market impact of large trades by hiding order information that might otherwise cause adverse price movements, but they also reduce the transparency that public price discovery relies upon.

The interaction between public exchanges and dark pools creates complex dynamics that can affect price discovery and execution quality for all market participants. When significant trading volume migrates to dark pools, the public exchanges may display less accurate information about supply and demand conditions, potentially leading to less efficient pricing for securities that trade heavily in private venues.

Electronic Communication Networks have further fragmented the traditional exchange model by providing alternative venues that match buyers and sellers directly without traditional market maker intermediation. These systems often provide lower transaction costs and faster execution for certain types of trades, but they also contribute to the complexity that modern market participants must navigate.

The regulatory framework governing market mechanics continues to evolve in response to technological changes and market structure developments. Rules governing best execution require brokers to seek the most favorable terms reasonably available for their customers' orders, but the complexity of modern markets makes it increasingly difficult to determine what constitutes best execution across multiple dimensions including price, speed, and execution probability.

Market makers operate under specific regulatory obligations that require them to provide continuous two-sided quotes during market hours while maintaining fair and orderly markets. These obligations help ensure liquidity availability for other market participants, but they also create risks for market makers who must continue quoting prices even during periods of extreme volatility or uncertainty.

Chapter 3: Building Your Investment Toolkit

3.1 Essential Valuation Tools and Analytical Frameworks

Successful investing requires more than intuition and market sentiment analysis. It demands a systematic approach built on proven analytical tools that can cut through market noise and identify genuine investment opportunities. The construction of a comprehensive investment toolkit involves mastering multiple valuation methodologies, understanding their appropriate applications, and recognizing their limitations. This analytical foundation provides the confidence necessary to make contrarian investment decisions when markets diverge from fundamental values.

The development of valuation expertise begins with understanding that no single metric or methodology provides complete insight into investment attractiveness. Different businesses require different analytical approaches based on their industry characteristics, growth stages, and competitive dynamics. Technology companies with minimal tangible assets but substantial intellectual property require fundamentally different evaluation techniques than real estate investment trusts or utility companies with substantial physical assets and predictable cash flows.

Price-to-earnings ratios represent the most widely used valuation metric, yet their apparent simplicity masks significant complexity in proper application and interpretation. The denominator in P/E calculations can vary dramatically based on whether analysts use trailing twelve-month earnings, forward-looking estimates, or normalized earnings that adjust for cyclical fluctuations. Each approach provides different insights and can lead to vastly different valuation conclusions for the same company.

Trailing P/E ratios based on historical earnings provide objective, verifiable data but may not reflect current business conditions or future prospects. Companies experiencing rapid growth or cyclical downturns often show misleading trailing P/E ratios that fail to capture their true earnings potential. Forward P/E ratios based on analyst estimates incorporate future expectations but depend on the accuracy of earnings forecasts that frequently prove optimistic or pessimistic.

The concept of normalized earnings becomes crucial when evaluating companies in cyclical industries where current earnings may be temporarily depressed or elevated relative to long-term averages. Steel companies, homebuilders, and commodity producers often trade at misleadingly low P/E ratios during cyclical peaks when earnings are temporarily elevated, while showing high P/E ratios during downturns when earnings are temporarily depressed.

Price-to-book ratios provide another fundamental valuation tool that measures market values relative to shareholders' equity, but their usefulness varies dramatically across different types of businesses. Asset-heavy industries like banking, real estate, and manufacturing often show meaningful relationships between book values and intrinsic values, making P/B ratios useful comparative tools. However, service businesses and technology companies with minimal tangible assets often trade at large premiums to book value that reflect intangible assets not captured in traditional accounting.

The quality of book value calculations significantly impacts P/B ratio analysis. Companies that have written down assets due to impairments or changed accounting standards may show artificially low book values that make P/B ratios appear elevated. Conversely, companies with substantial hidden asset values due to conservative accounting or historical cost accounting may show understated book values that make P/B ratios appear attractively low.

Return on equity analysis provides crucial context for P/B ratio interpretation by revealing how efficiently companies utilize shareholders' capital to generate profits. Companies with consistently high ROE often deserve premium valuations relative to book value, while companies with low or declining ROE may be fairly valued despite appearing cheap on P/B ratio analysis.

Enterprise value to EBITDA ratios offer a more comprehensive valuation framework that accounts for different capital structures while focusing on operating performance. Enterprise value calculations add market capitalization to net debt, providing a measure of total company value that enables comparisons between companies with different financing strategies. EBITDA removes the effects of depreciation, amortization, interest, and taxes to focus on core operating performance.

The EV/EBITDA framework proves particularly valuable for comparing companies across industries or evaluating acquisition candidates where new owners might implement different financing or tax strategies. However, EBITDA's exclusion of capital expenditures can be misleading for businesses that require substantial ongoing investments to maintain their competitive positions.

Cash flow-based valuation methods provide the most theoretically sound approach to investment analysis by focusing on the actual cash that businesses generate for their owners. Discounted cash flow analysis attempts to estimate the present value of all future cash flows that a business will generate, discounted back to current dollars using an appropriate cost of capital.

DCF analysis requires making explicit assumptions about future growth rates, profit margins, capital requirements, and terminal values that extend far into the future. These long-term projections necessarily involve substantial uncertainty, making DCF analysis as much art as science. However, the process of building detailed financial models forces analysts to understand business fundamentals in ways that simple ratio analysis cannot achieve.

The terminal value calculation often represents the largest component of DCF valuations, as the majority of a company's value typically derives from cash flows beyond the detailed forecast period. Terminal value estimates using perpetual growth rates or exit multiples can dramatically impact overall valuations, making it crucial to test various scenarios and understand the sensitivity of conclusions to different assumptions.

Relative valuation approaches compare companies to industry peers or historical trading ranges rather than attempting to calculate intrinsic values. These methods assume that markets generally price similar companies at similar multiples, making outliers potentially attractive investment opportunities. However, relative valuation can perpetuate market-wide overvaluation or undervaluation if entire sectors become mispriced.

Industry-specific metrics often provide more relevant comparisons than generic financial ratios. Retail companies might be valued based on sales per square foot or same-store sales growth, while subscription businesses focus on customer acquisition costs and lifetime value metrics. Understanding these specialized metrics becomes essential for analyzing companies in particular sectors.

Hidden asset identification represents one of the most rewarding aspects of fundamental analysis, requiring detective work to uncover values that don't appear prominently in financial statements. Real estate held at historical cost often trades for multiples of book value, particularly for companies that have owned properties for decades in appreciating markets. Restaurant chains, retailers, and industrial companies frequently own valuable real estate that could be monetized through sale-leaseback transactions or redevelopment.

Patent portfolios and intellectual property can represent substantial hidden values that traditional accounting doesn't capture. Technology companies that have developed proprietary technologies internally carry these assets at minimal book values despite their potentially enormous licensing or strategic value. Pharmaceutical companies with expiring patents may possess early-stage drug development programs that could prove valuable but don't appear in current financial metrics.

Brand value represents another category of hidden assets that can provide sustainable competitive advantages and pricing power not reflected in tangible asset values. Consumer products companies with strong brand recognition often generate premium returns on invested capital that justify higher valuations than commodity businesses, but quantifying brand values requires subjective judgment about customer loyalty and pricing power sustainability.

Working capital efficiency analysis reveals companies that generate cash while growing their businesses, indicating superior operational management and attractive investment characteristics. Companies that can grow revenues while reducing working capital as a percentage of sales essentially get paid to expand, creating powerful cash generation that funds further growth or shareholder returns.

The cash conversion cycle measures how long companies take to convert inventory investments into cash collections, providing insights into operational efficiency and cash flow generation. Companies with negative cash conversion cycles collect cash from customers before paying suppliers, creating float that can be invested profitably while maintaining operations.

Walmart's ability to collect cash from customers immediately while paying suppliers on extended terms creates enormous float that the company invests to generate additional returns. This working capital advantage provides a sustainable competitive advantage that becomes apparent through cash flow analysis but might not be obvious from traditional profitability metrics.

Off-balance-sheet obligation analysis requires careful examination of footnotes and regulatory filings to identify hidden liabilities that could significantly impact future cash flows. Operating lease commitments, pension obligations, and contingent liabilities might not appear prominently in balance sheet presentations but represent substantial future cash requirements that affect investment attractiveness.

The recent changes in lease accounting standards that require companies to recognize operating leases as liabilities provide better transparency into total debt burdens, but historical analysis requires manual adjustments to understand true leverage levels. Airlines, retailers, and restaurant companies that extensively use operating leases often carry substantially more debt than traditional balance sheet presentations suggest.

3.2 Technology and Automation

The democratization of investment technology has fundamentally altered the landscape for individual investors, providing access to sophisticated analytical tools and real-time data that were previously available only to institutional investors with substantial budgets. The key to leveraging this technological revolution lies not in adopting every available tool, but in strategically selecting and mastering the technologies that align with your investment approach and analytical needs.

Modern portfolio management software has evolved far beyond simple spreadsheet tracking to provide comprehensive analytical capabilities that rival professional-grade systems. Platforms like Personal Capital and Mint offer automated portfolio analysis that tracks asset allocation, calculates fees across multiple accounts, and provides performance attribution analysis that helps investors understand which investments are contributing to or detracting from overall returns. These systems automatically sync with brokerage accounts, banks, and other financial institutions to provide real-time portfolio monitoring without manual data entry.

The sophistication of these platforms extends to tax optimization features that can identify opportunities for tax-loss harvesting, asset location optimization across taxable and tax-advantaged accounts, and withdrawal strategies that minimize tax implications during retirement. Advanced users can customize these systems to implement complex investment strategies while maintaining automated monitoring and rebalancing capabilities.

Screening and research platforms have become increasingly powerful while remaining accessible to individual investors. Services like Finviz, Yahoo Finance, and Google Finance provide sophisticated stock screening capabilities that allow investors to filter thousands of securities based on multiple financial metrics, technical indicators, and fundamental criteria simultaneously. These screens can identify value opportunities, growth stocks, dividend aristocrats, or any other investment criteria that align with specific investment strategies.

The key to effective screening lies in understanding how to construct meaningful filters that identify genuinely attractive opportunities while avoiding false positives that appear attractive based on misleading metrics. For example, screening for low price-to-earnings ratios without considering debt levels or earnings quality might identify distressed companies with artificially depressed earnings rather than genuine value opportunities.

Backtesting capabilities within these platforms allow investors to test investment strategies against historical data to understand how they would have performed under different market conditions. While past performance doesn't guarantee future results, backtesting provides valuable insights into strategy behavior during various market cycles and helps investors understand the risk-return characteristics of different approaches.

Artificial intelligence and machine learning tools are increasingly available to individual investors through various platforms and applications. These systems can analyze vast amounts of unstructured data including news articles, social media sentiment, satellite imagery, and economic indicators to identify patterns and trends that human analysts might miss. However, the effectiveness of these tools depends heavily on the quality of underlying data and the sophistication of the algorithms, making it crucial to understand their limitations and validate their outputs through traditional analysis.

Robo-advisors represent one of the most successful applications of investment automation for individual investors, providing professionally designed portfolio management at a fraction of the cost of traditional investment advisors. These platforms use modern portfolio theory and sophisticated optimization algorithms to construct diversified portfolios tailored to individual risk tolerance and investment objectives.

The most advanced robo-advisors incorporate tax-loss harvesting, automatic rebalancing, and goal-based investing features that continuously optimize portfolios based on changing market conditions and individual circumstances. Some platforms now offer direct indexing capabilities that allow investors to own individual stocks rather than mutual funds or ETFs while maintaining diversification and tax efficiency.

However, robo-advisors typically work best for investors with straightforward financial situations and investment goals. Complex situations involving business ownership, real estate investments, or unique tax circumstances often require human expertise that automated systems cannot provide.

Alternative data sources powered by technology provide individual investors with insights that were previously available only to sophisticated institutional investors. Satellite imagery analysis can provide early indicators of economic activity, crop yields, or retail foot traffic that precede official economic statistics. Social media sentiment analysis can identify emerging trends or changing consumer preferences that might impact specific companies or sectors.

Credit card transaction data, when aggregated and anonymized, provides real-time insights into consumer spending patterns that can help investors anticipate earnings surprises or identify changing competitive dynamics within retail sectors. However, accessing and interpreting this data requires substantial technological sophistication and often involves significant costs that may not be justified for smaller investment portfolios.

Mobile applications have made sophisticated investment tools available anywhere with internet connectivity, allowing investors to monitor positions, execute trades, and conduct research from any location. Advanced mobile platforms provide full-featured charting capabilities, options trading, and research tools that rival desktop applications.

The convenience of mobile investing creates both opportunities and risks for individual investors. While mobile access enables quick responses to market opportunities, it also facilitates impulsive trading decisions that might not align with long-term investment strategies. Successful mobile investing requires the discipline to use convenient access for monitoring and research rather than frequent trading.

Automated investing strategies can help investors maintain discipline by removing emotional decision-making from routine investment activities. Dollar-cost averaging programs automatically invest predetermined amounts at regular intervals regardless of market conditions, helping investors avoid the timing mistakes that often undermine investment returns. Automatic rebalancing ensures that portfolio allocations remain aligned with target percentages as market movements cause drift over time.

The key to successful investment automation lies in setting up systems that support long-term investment objectives while providing flexibility to adjust strategies as circumstances change. Over-automation can prevent investors from taking advantage of opportunities or responding to changing conditions, while under-automation might allow emotional decision-making to undermine systematic investment approaches.

3.3 Essential Free Resources

Professional investors collectively spend over thirty billion dollars annually on research tools, data feeds, and analytical platforms, yet individual investors can access approximately eighty percent of the same fundamental information through free or low-cost resources. The key advantage lies not in having access to exclusive information, but in knowing where to find reliable data and how to interpret it effectively.

The Securities and Exchange Commission's EDGAR database represents the most comprehensive source of corporate financial information available to investors, containing every public filing that companies are required to submit. Understanding how to navigate and extract value from EDGAR filings provides individual investors with the same fundamental information that professional analysts use to make investment decisions, often before this information gets summarized and interpreted by financial media.

Form 10-K annual reports contain the most comprehensive overview of a company's business operations, financial condition, and risk factors. These documents typically run hundreds of pages and include detailed discussions of competitive dynamics, regulatory challenges, and management's assessment of future prospects that rarely appear in abbreviated earnings announcements or analyst reports. The Management

Discussion and Analysis section provides particularly valuable insights into how executives view their business challenges and opportunities.

Form 10-Q quarterly reports provide updates on financial performance and significant developments that have occurred since the last annual report. While these documents receive less attention than earnings announcements, they often contain detailed explanations of unusual items, accounting changes, or business developments that can significantly impact investment decisions.

Proxy statements filed as DEF 14A documents reveal crucial information about executive compensation, board composition, and significant shareholder proposals that can indicate potential conflicts of interest or alignment between management and shareholder interests. These filings often disclose related-party transactions, executive stock option grants, and other arrangements that might not be apparent from financial statements alone.

Form 8-K current reports announce material events or corporate changes that occur between regular reporting periods. These filings cover everything from acquisition announcements and management changes to accounting restatements and legal proceedings. Learning to monitor 8-K filings provides early access to important corporate developments that can significantly impact stock prices.

Insider trading reports filed as Forms 3, 4, and 5 reveal when corporate executives, directors, and significant shareholders buy or sell company stock. While individual transactions might reflect personal financial planning rather than investment views, patterns of insider buying or selling can provide valuable insights into management's confidence in company prospects.

The key to effective EDGAR analysis lies in understanding how to quickly identify the most relevant sections of lengthy documents while recognizing potential red flags that warrant deeper investigation. Learning to use EDGAR's search functions and RSS feeds allows investors to monitor multiple companies efficiently and receive automatic notifications when important filings become available.

Economic data dashboards provided by government agencies offer comprehensive access to macroeconomic statistics that professional investors pay substantial fees to receive from private data vendors. The Federal Reserve Economic Data platform, known as FRED, provides access to over 800,000 economic time series covering everything from employment statistics and inflation measures to international trade data and monetary policy indicators.

Understanding how to interpret and apply economic data requires recognizing the relationships between different economic indicators and their potential impact on various investment sectors. Employment statistics affect consumer discretionary companies differently than industrial firms, while inflation measures have varying implications for real estate investment trusts, fixed-income securities, and commodity-related investments.

The Bureau of Labor Statistics provides detailed employment, wage, and price data that can help investors anticipate economic trends and sector rotation opportunities. Regional employment statistics can identify geographic areas experiencing economic growth or decline that might impact locally-focused businesses or real estate investments.

The Census Bureau publishes comprehensive demographic and economic data that provides context for long-term investment themes. Population growth patterns, household formation trends, and income distribution changes can help investors identify sectors likely to benefit from demographic shifts over extended periods.

International economic data sources provide insights into global trends and opportunities that affect multinational corporations and emerging market investments. The Organization for Economic Cooperation and Development publishes comparative economic statistics across developed countries, while the International Monetary Fund provides comprehensive data on emerging market economies.

Industry-specific databases maintained by trade associations and government agencies often provide more detailed and timely information about particular sectors than generic financial databases. The American Petroleum Institute publishes weekly oil inventory data that professional traders pay significant fees to access through private services, yet this same information is available for free directly from the source.

The Federal Aviation Administration publishes detailed airline traffic statistics that provide insights into industry trends and individual carrier performance. The Association of American Railroads provides rail traffic data that can help investors understand economic activity and commodity demand patterns. These specialized data sources often provide earlier indicators of industry trends than quarterly earnings reports.

State and local government databases provide valuable information about regional economic conditions and industry-specific trends. State revenue departments publish tax collection data that can indicate economic activity levels, while local planning departments provide building permit and zoning information that can help evaluate real estate investment opportunities.

University research databases provide access to academic studies and analytical frameworks that can enhance investment decision-making. Many universities publish industry studies, economic forecasts, and investment research that rivals the quality of professional research reports. Understanding how to access and evaluate academic research can provide unique perspectives on investment opportunities and risks.

The key to leveraging free information resources lies in developing systematic processes for monitoring relevant data sources while filtering out noise that doesn't impact investment decisions. Creating custom alerts and RSS feeds for specific companies, economic indicators, or industry data allows investors to stay informed without becoming overwhelmed by information overload.

Successful utilization of free resources also requires understanding their limitations compared to premium services. Free data often has slight delays compared to real-time professional feeds, and free research tools may lack some advanced analytical capabilities available in expensive professional platforms. However, for most individual investment strategies, these limitations don't significantly impact decision-making quality or investment outcomes.

Chapter 4: The Art of Stock Selection

4.1 Understanding Stock Selection Fundamentals

Stock selection represents both the most challenging and potentially rewarding aspect of individual investing, requiring the synthesis of analytical skills, psychological discipline, and strategic thinking that distinguishes successful investors from those who struggle to achieve satisfactory returns. Unlike passive index investing, which accepts market returns while minimizing costs and complexity, active stock selection demands that investors develop the capability to identify securities that are mispriced relative to their intrinsic values and possess the patience to wait for markets to recognize these discrepancies.

The foundation of effective stock selection begins with recognizing that successful investing is fundamentally about buying pieces of businesses rather than trading abstract financial instruments. This ownership perspective transforms stock selection from a speculative exercise focused on predicting short-term price movements into a systematic evaluation of business quality, competitive position, and long-term value creation potential. Understanding this distinction proves crucial because it shapes every subsequent aspect of the investment process, from initial screening criteria to holding period decisions.

The concept of intrinsic value serves as the cornerstone of rational stock selection, providing an objective framework for determining whether securities are attractively priced relative to their underlying business values. Intrinsic value represents the present value of all future cash flows that a business will generate for its owners, discounted back to current dollars using an appropriate rate of return that reflects the risks inherent in the investment. While calculating precise intrinsic values requires making assumptions about uncertain future conditions, the process of estimating these values forces investors to think systematically about business fundamentals and long-term prospects.

The relationship between market prices and intrinsic values creates the opportunities that skilled stock selectors seek to exploit. When market prices trade below calculated intrinsic values, securities offer positive expected returns that compensate investors for the risks they assume. Conversely, when market prices exceed intrinsic values, securities become poor investments regardless of how attractive the underlying businesses might appear from a qualitative perspective.

However, successful stock selection requires more than simply identifying securities trading below estimated intrinsic values. Investors must also consider the quality of the businesses they are purchasing, the sustainability of competitive advantages, and the likelihood that intrinsic values will grow over time. A stock trading at fifty percent of its intrinsic value represents a poor investment if that intrinsic value is declining due to technological obsolescence or competitive pressures, while a stock trading at ninety percent of intrinsic value might prove excellent if the underlying business is growing rapidly and strengthening its competitive position.

The time horizon consideration fundamentally shapes stock selection criteria and influences the types of businesses that prove most attractive for different investment strategies. Short-term oriented investors might focus on companies experiencing temporary setbacks that depress market prices below intrinsic values, betting that markets will recognize these discrepancies within relatively brief periods. Long-term oriented investors can afford to emphasize business quality and growth potential over immediate price dislocations, accepting current market prices that approximate intrinsic values in exchange for businesses capable of growing their intrinsic values substantially over extended periods.

Understanding your natural investment time horizon becomes crucial because it determines which stock selection approaches are likely to succeed and which are likely to generate frustration and poor results. Investors with short attention spans or immediate income needs should avoid strategies that require extended holding periods to realize their potential, while investors with long time horizons can pursue strategies that might take years to demonstrate their effectiveness.

The concept of margin of safety provides essential protection against the inevitable errors in judgment and unforeseen circumstances that affect all investment decisions. Benjamin Graham popularized this principle by advocating purchases only when market prices offered substantial discounts to estimated intrinsic values, providing cushions that could absorb analytical mistakes or temporary business setbacks without causing permanent capital losses. The appropriate margin of safety varies based on the certainty of intrinsic value estimates and the quality of the underlying businesses, with higher margins required for uncertain situations and lower margins acceptable for high-quality, predictable companies.

Circle of competence represents another fundamental principle that successful stock selectors must embrace to avoid costly mistakes in industries or business models they don't understand. Warren Buffett has consistently emphasized the importance of staying within areas of expertise rather than venturing into complex or unfamiliar businesses that might appear attractive but involve risks that investors cannot properly evaluate. Developing deep expertise in particular industries or business models allows investors to recognize subtleties and competitive dynamics that generalist approaches might miss.

The process of defining and expanding your circle of competence requires honest self-assessment about your knowledge base and experience while committing to continuous learning about the industries and companies you choose to focus on. Some investors develop expertise in consumer products companies by leveraging their understanding of brands and customer behavior, while others focus on technology companies where their professional experience provides analytical advantages. The specific area of expertise matters less than genuine depth of understanding and commitment to staying current with industry developments.

Business model analysis forms a crucial component of stock selection that goes beyond traditional financial metrics to understand how companies create and capture value. Different business models possess vastly different characteristics in terms of scalability, predictability, competitive defensibility, and capital requirements that significantly impact their investment attractiveness. Subscription-based software companies with high switching costs and recurring revenue streams possess fundamentally different investment characteristics than cyclical manufacturing companies that compete primarily on price.

Understanding business model dynamics helps investors identify companies with sustainable competitive advantages that can generate superior returns on invested capital over extended periods. These advantages might stem from network effects that make products more valuable as more customers use them, economies of scale that reduce per-unit costs as volumes increase, or brand loyalty that allows premium pricing compared to generic alternatives.

The evaluation of management quality represents one of the most challenging yet important aspects of stock selection, as management decisions ultimately determine whether businesses realize their potential or squander competitive advantages through poor capital allocation or strategic missteps. Assessing management quality requires examining track records of value creation, communication transparency, capital allocation decisions, and alignment of interests between management and shareholders.

Management track records provide objective evidence of decision-making quality over extended periods, revealing patterns of value creation or destruction that tend to persist over time. Managers who have consistently grown intrinsic value per share through organic growth, acquisitions, or capital allocation generally deserve premium valuations compared to managers with records of destroying shareholder value through poor investments or excessive compensation.

The assessment of management communication quality involves evaluating whether executives provide honest, comprehensive information about business conditions, competitive challenges, and strategic priorities. Managers who consistently provide accurate guidance, acknowledge mistakes honestly, and explain their decision-making rationale generally prove more trustworthy than those who consistently paint overly optimistic pictures or blame external factors for poor performance.

Capital allocation evaluation examines how management deploys the cash flows generated by their businesses, as these decisions often determine whether companies create or destroy shareholder value over time. Excellent managers allocate capital to the highest returning opportunities available, whether through reinvestment in the business, acquisitions, debt reduction, or returns to shareholders through dividends and share repurchases.

Industry analysis provides essential context for stock selection by revealing structural characteristics that influence competitive dynamics, profitability levels, and growth prospects for all participants within particular sectors. Some industries possess characteristics that make sustained profitability difficult for most participants, while others offer attractive dynamics that benefit well-positioned companies. Understanding these industry-level factors helps investors avoid structural value traps while identifying sectors where stock selection skills can add the most value.

Cyclical industry analysis requires particular sophistication to avoid buying apparent bargains at peak earnings levels or selling quality companies during temporary downturns. Companies in industries like steel, chemicals, and homebuilding often show misleadingly attractive valuations based on peak cycle earnings that prove unsustainable once supply and demand rebalance. Successful investing in cyclical industries requires understanding normal cycle patterns and positioning for recovery phases rather than chasing momentum during peak periods.

Growth industry analysis involves identifying sectors benefiting from long-term secular trends while avoiding the valuation excesses that often accompany rapidly growing markets. Technology, healthcare, and renewable energy represent examples of industries that have generated substantial wealth for early investors but also created numerous disappointments for those who paid excessive prices or selected inferior companies within attractive sectors.

The integration of quantitative and qualitative analysis provides the most comprehensive foundation for stock selection decisions, combining objective financial metrics with subjective assessments of business quality and competitive position. Quantitative analysis provides standardized frameworks for comparing different investment opportunities while identifying potential red flags that warrant deeper investigation. Qualitative analysis provides context and nuance that pure financial metrics cannot capture, revealing the sustainable competitive advantages and management capabilities that drive long-term value creation.

Successful stock selection requires developing systematic processes that can be applied consistently while remaining flexible enough to adapt to changing market conditions and new opportunities. These processes should incorporate both screening mechanisms that identify potentially attractive opportunities and evaluation frameworks that can thoroughly assess the investment merits of individual securities. The goal is to develop an approach that maximizes the probability of success while minimizing the potential for costly mistakes that could permanently impair investment capital.

4.2 Company Evaluation Framework

Peter Lynch achieved twenty-nine percent annual returns over thirteen years by investing in companies he encountered in daily life, demonstrating that unique personal perspectives and experiences can provide significant investment advantages over sophisticated analytical models that miss obvious trends unfolding in plain sight. This approach to company evaluation emphasizes the importance of combining systematic analytical frameworks with observational insights that come from understanding how businesses actually operate in the real world.

The foundation of effective company evaluation begins with recognizing that investment opportunities often emerge from major societal shifts that create new demands, disrupt existing business models, or alter competitive landscapes in ways that benefit certain companies while disadvantaging others. These megatrends typically develop over years or decades, providing patient investors with multiple opportunities to identify and invest in companies positioned to benefit from long-term structural changes.

Demographic megatrends represent some of the most predictable and powerful forces shaping investment opportunities across multiple decades. The aging of populations in developed countries creates enormous opportunities for companies serving healthcare needs, retirement planning, and age-related services while potentially challenging businesses that depend on younger consumer demographics. The scope of this demographic shift extends far beyond obvious healthcare investments to include housing patterns, transportation preferences, entertainment choices, and financial services that cater to changing life stage needs.

The global trend toward urbanization creates investment opportunities in companies that facilitate city living, including real estate development, public transportation, urban agriculture, and digital services that help manage complex city life. As rural populations migrate to urban centers worldwide, the resulting infrastructure needs, housing demands, and lifestyle changes create multi-decade investment themes that benefit companies positioned to serve these emerging needs.

Identifying companies that can capitalize on demographic trends requires understanding both the magnitude and timing of these shifts while recognizing which businesses possess the capabilities and competitive positions necessary to capture the resulting opportunities. Healthcare companies serving aging populations must demonstrate not only exposure to growing markets but also competitive advantages in research and development, regulatory navigation, or service delivery that enable them to succeed against existing competitors and new entrants attracted by growth opportunities.

Technological disruption patterns provide another rich source of investment opportunities for investors who can recognize industry transformation early in the process, before stock prices fully reflect the potential for change. The key to profiting from technological disruption lies in understanding that technology adoption typically follows predictable patterns while the pace and ultimate impact often exceed initial expectations.

The evolution of digital transformation across traditional industries illustrates how technological disruption creates winners and losers in ways that aren't immediately obvious to casual observers. Companies that successfully integrate digital technologies into their operations often gain significant competitive advantages through improved efficiency, better customer experiences, or new revenue opportunities. Meanwhile, companies that resist or poorly implement digital transformation frequently find themselves at increasing disadvantages that compound over time.

Cloud computing represents a multi-decade technological shift that continues to create investment opportunities as more businesses migrate from traditional on-premises systems to cloud-based solutions. This transition benefits not only the major cloud infrastructure providers but also software companies that design applications for cloud deployment, cybersecurity firms that protect cloud-based systems, and consulting companies that help businesses navigate the transition.

Artificial intelligence and machine learning technologies are following similar adoption patterns, creating opportunities for companies that can successfully integrate these capabilities into practical business applications while avoiding the hype cycles that often accompany emerging technologies. The most attractive investment opportunities typically involve companies that use artificial intelligence to solve specific business problems rather than those that simply claim artificial intelligence capabilities without clear value propositions.

Consumer behavior shifts often provide the earliest and most visible indicators of changing business prospects for companies serving retail markets. Observant investors can identify these shifts through their own experiences and observations while traditional Wall Street analysis focuses on historical financial metrics that may not capture emerging trends until they significantly impact reported results.

The evolution of consumer shopping patterns toward online purchasing created enormous opportunities for e-commerce companies while challenging traditional retailers, but the specific winners and losers within these categories weren't immediately obvious. Success required identifying companies with superior logistics capabilities, customer acquisition strategies, and operational efficiency rather than simply betting on all online retailers or against all traditional stores.

Changing food preferences toward healthier, more sustainable options create opportunities for companies producing organic foods, plant-based proteins, and environmentally friendly packaging while potentially challenging traditional food manufacturers that resist adapting their product lines. These trends often begin with smaller, niche companies before affecting larger industry participants, providing opportunities for investors who identify promising smaller companies before they achieve mainstream recognition.

The shift toward experiences over material possessions particularly among younger demographics creates opportunities for companies in travel, entertainment, dining, and experiential retail while potentially challenging traditional goods manufacturers. Understanding these preference shifts requires recognizing that different demographic cohorts often maintain distinct consumption patterns throughout their lifetimes rather than simply adopting the preferences of previous generations as they age.

Evaluating companies within the context of these broader trends requires developing frameworks that can assess both the magnitude of the opportunity and the specific company's ability to capitalize on it successfully. Market size analysis helps determine whether trends are significant enough to drive meaningful business growth, while competitive position analysis evaluates whether particular companies possess the advantages necessary to capture disproportionate shares of growing markets.

The timing of investment decisions relative to trend development significantly impacts potential returns, as early-stage investments in emerging trends often involve higher risks but offer greater upside potential, while later-stage investments in established trends typically offer more predictable but modest returns. Understanding where particular trends stand in their development cycles helps determine appropriate risk-adjusted return expectations and position sizing decisions.

Sustainable competitive advantage assessment becomes crucial when evaluating companies positioned to benefit from long-term trends, as the presence of structural advantages often determines whether companies can maintain profitable growth as trends mature and competition intensifies. Network effects, switching costs, economies of scale, and regulatory barriers can protect advantaged companies from competitive pressures that often emerge as attractive markets develop.

Management evaluation takes on particular importance when assessing companies operating in rapidly changing environments, as leadership quality often determines whether organizations can successfully navigate the opportunities and challenges that accompany major trends. Successful management teams demonstrate adaptability, strategic vision, and execution capabilities that enable them to evolve their businesses as underlying trends develop and competitive conditions change.

4.3 Portfolio Construction and Risk Management

The translation of individual stock selection decisions into coherent portfolio construction requires systematic approaches that balance potential returns with risk management while ensuring that overall portfolio characteristics align with investment objectives and personal circumstances. Effective portfolio construction goes beyond simply assembling collections of attractive individual investments to create synergistic combinations that can achieve superior risk-adjusted returns through diversification, correlation management, and strategic asset allocation.

Position sizing represents one of the most critical yet often overlooked aspects of portfolio construction, as the allocation of capital among different investments ultimately determines portfolio performance more than the selection of individual securities. Even excellent stock selection cannot overcome poor position sizing decisions that concentrate too much capital in high-risk investments or spread resources so thinly that successful investments cannot meaningfully impact overall returns.

The Kelly Criterion provides a mathematical framework for optimal position sizing based on the probability of success and potential payoff ratios of individual investments. While precise Kelly Criterion calculations require probability estimates that are difficult to determine with confidence, the underlying principles help investors think systematically about how much capital to allocate to different opportunities based on their risk-reward characteristics.

Practical position sizing approaches often use simpler rules that limit individual positions to predetermined percentages of total portfolio value while allowing larger allocations for higher-conviction investments with better risk-reward profiles. Many successful investors limit individual stock positions to between two and eight percent of portfolio value, with larger allocations reserved for their highest-conviction ideas and smaller positions used for more speculative or uncertain investments.

Diversification strategies must balance the risk reduction benefits of spreading investments across multiple securities with the concentration necessary to benefit meaningfully from successful stock selection. Over-diversification can eliminate the advantages of superior stock selection by reducing portfolio returns toward market averages, while under-diversification can expose portfolios to unacceptable risks from individual company or sector-specific problems.

Effective diversification requires understanding the different types of risks that affect investment portfolios and ensuring adequate protection against each category. Company-specific risks can be reduced through owning multiple individual securities, while sector concentration risks require spreading investments across different industries and business models. Geographic diversification provides protection against country-specific economic or political risks, while currency diversification can reduce exposure to specific monetary policy decisions.

Correlation analysis helps optimize diversification effectiveness by identifying investments that behave differently during various market conditions, providing natural hedges that can reduce overall portfolio volatility without sacrificing expected returns. Low or negative correlations between different investments enhance diversification benefits, while high positive correlations reduce diversification effectiveness and may indicate inadequate risk spreading.

Risk budgeting approaches allocate portfolio risk capacity among different investments and strategies rather than simply allocating capital, recognizing that some investments contribute more risk than others regardless of their dollar allocations. High-volatility growth stocks might warrant smaller capital allocations than stable dividend-paying companies to achieve similar risk contributions to overall portfolio volatility.

Rebalancing strategies maintain intended portfolio allocations as market movements cause individual positions to grow or shrink relative to target weightings. Systematic rebalancing forces investors to sell portions of investments that have become overweighted and purchase additional shares of investments that have become underweighted, implementing a disciplined buy-low, sell-high approach that can enhance long-term returns.

The frequency and methodology of rebalancing significantly impact transaction costs and tax implications while influencing portfolio performance characteristics. More frequent rebalancing reduces allocation drift but increases transaction costs and potential tax consequences, while less frequent rebalancing allows greater allocation drift but reduces implementation costs.

Tax management considerations become particularly important for portfolios held in taxable accounts, as tax-efficient strategies can significantly enhance after-tax returns over extended periods. Tax-loss harvesting involves selling investments at losses to offset taxable gains from successful investments, while tax-efficient fund selection and asset location strategies can minimize ongoing tax drag on portfolio performance.

Risk monitoring systems help investors track portfolio risk characteristics and identify potential problems before they cause significant losses. Value-at-risk calculations estimate potential portfolio losses during adverse market conditions, while stress testing evaluates portfolio behavior during various economic scenarios that might challenge underlying assumptions.

Scenario analysis examines how portfolios might perform during different economic conditions, market environments, or industry-specific challenges that could affect multiple holdings simultaneously. Understanding portfolio sensitivity to interest rate changes, inflation variations, economic recessions, or geopolitical events helps investors prepare for various contingencies and adjust allocations when risk levels become unacceptable.

The integration of individual security analysis with portfolio-level risk management creates comprehensive investment processes that can achieve superior long-term results while avoiding the concentration risks and systematic biases that often undermine otherwise sound investment approaches. Success requires maintaining discipline in both stock selection and portfolio construction while remaining flexible enough to adapt to changing market conditions and personal circumstances.

Chapter 5: Portfolio Architecture and Risk Management

A comprehensive analysis of retirement accounts revealed that proper asset allocation explained over ninety percent of portfolio returns, while individual security selection contributed less than five percent to performance outcomes. This striking finding underscores one of the most important yet often overlooked principles in investment management: building the right portfolio structure matters significantly more than picking individual winners. The architecture of your portfolio - how you combine different asset classes, manage correlations, and maintain strategic allocations - ultimately determines your investment success far more than your ability to identify the next great stock or time market movements.

5.1 Strategic Asset Allocation

Strategic asset allocation represents the foundation upon which all other investment decisions rest, establishing the basic framework that determines portfolio risk and return characteristics over extended periods. Unlike tactical decisions about individual securities or market timing, strategic allocation focuses on the long-term mix of asset classes that can best achieve your investment objectives while remaining compatible with your risk tolerance and time horizon.

The power of strategic asset allocation stems from its ability to harness the fundamental risk-return relationships that exist between different asset classes while managing the correlations that determine how these assets behave together during various market conditions. By thoughtfully combining assets with different return characteristics and correlation patterns, investors can potentially achieve superior risk-adjusted returns compared to portfolios concentrated in any single asset class.

Understanding the historical risk and return characteristics of major asset classes provides the foundation for making informed strategic allocation decisions. Large-cap domestic stocks have historically provided higher returns than bonds over extended periods, but with significantly higher volatility that can challenge investors' ability to maintain their positions during adverse periods. Small-cap stocks have generally offered higher returns than large-cap stocks, but with even greater volatility that requires strong conviction and long time horizons to realize their potential benefits.

International developed market stocks provide diversification benefits relative to domestic holdings, though these benefits have diminished somewhat as global markets have become increasingly correlated during crisis periods. Emerging market stocks offer potentially higher returns but with substantially higher volatility and political risks that require careful consideration within overall portfolio context.

Fixed-income securities traditionally provide stability and income that can offset equity volatility, though their return potential has been limited during periods of low interest rates. Treasury bonds offer the highest credit quality and negative correlation with stocks during most market stress periods, while corporate bonds provide higher yields at the cost of increased credit risk. International bonds add currency diversification but introduce additional complexity and risks.

Alternative asset classes including real estate, commodities, and hedge fund strategies can provide additional diversification benefits, though they often involve higher costs, lower liquidity, and greater complexity that may not be appropriate for all investors. The decision to include alternative investments should be based on their specific risk-return characteristics and correlation benefits rather than simply pursuing diversification for its own sake.

Core-satellite approach: Balancing index funds with active selections

The core-satellite approach represents a sophisticated portfolio construction strategy that combines the reliability and cost-effectiveness of passive index investing with the potential return enhancement of active security selection. This framework recognizes that different portions of a portfolio serve different purposes and can be managed using different strategies that optimize the overall risk-return profile.

The core component typically consists of low-cost, broad-based index funds that provide market exposure across major asset classes while minimizing costs and tracking error relative to market benchmarks. This foundation ensures that the portfolio captures broad market returns while providing the stability and predictability that enable long-term financial planning. Core holdings might include total stock market index funds, international developed market funds, and broad bond market funds that collectively provide exposure to the major sources of investment returns.

The satellite component allows for active management strategies that can potentially enhance returns or provide specialized exposure that core holdings cannot deliver. Satellite positions might include individual stock selections, sector-specific funds, emerging market allocations, or alternative investment strategies that offer the potential for superior returns while accepting higher risks and costs.

The optimal balance between core and satellite allocations depends on individual circumstances, investment expertise, and risk tolerance. Conservative investors might allocate eighty to ninety percent of their portfolios to core holdings with small satellite positions in specialized strategies. More aggressive investors with greater investment knowledge might reverse this allocation, using index funds as stability anchors while pursuing active strategies with the majority of their assets.

The core-satellite approach provides several important advantages over purely passive or purely active strategies. The core component ensures broad market participation that prevents missing major market advances due to poor active management decisions. The satellite component allows for expression of investment insights and specialized exposure that can enhance returns or provide risk management benefits that broad market exposure cannot deliver.

Implementation of core-satellite strategies requires disciplined adherence to predetermined allocation targets while maintaining flexibility to adjust satellite positions based on changing opportunities and market conditions. The core positions should remain relatively stable over time, providing the foundational exposure that supports long-term investment objectives. Satellite positions can be more dynamic, allowing for tactical adjustments and opportunistic investments that take advantage of changing market conditions.

Risk management within core-satellite frameworks requires ensuring that satellite positions don't overwhelm the stability provided by core holdings. Even when satellite positions perform poorly, the core component should provide sufficient stability to prevent unacceptable portfolio volatility that could force abandonment of the long-term strategy.

Correlation analysis: Building portfolios that zig when markets zag

Correlation analysis forms the mathematical foundation of modern portfolio theory by quantifying how different investments move relative to each other during various market conditions. Understanding and managing correlations enables investors to construct portfolios that can potentially reduce risk without proportionally reducing expected returns, achieving the diversification benefits that represent the closest thing to a free lunch in investing.

Correlation coefficients range from negative one to positive one, with perfect positive correlation meaning that two investments always move in the same direction, perfect negative correlation meaning they always move in opposite directions, and zero correlation indicating no relationship between their price movements. In practice, most asset correlations fall somewhere between zero and positive one, with perfect correlations being extremely rare in real markets.

The power of correlation analysis becomes apparent when combining assets with low or negative correlations into portfolio structures. Two assets with identical expected returns and risk levels can create a portfolio with the same expected return but lower risk when combined if their correlation is less than perfect positive. This risk reduction benefit increases as correlations decrease, reaching maximum effectiveness when correlations approach negative one.

However, correlation relationships are not static and tend to change during different market conditions, with most asset correlations increasing during crisis periods when diversification benefits are needed most. The 2008 financial crisis demonstrated this phenomenon as previously uncorrelated assets like stocks, bonds, commodities, and real estate all declined simultaneously, temporarily eliminating many traditional diversification benefits.

Understanding correlation dynamics requires examining relationships across different time periods and market conditions rather than relying solely on long-term historical averages. Correlations during normal market conditions often differ significantly from correlations during crisis periods, making it important to stress-test portfolio structures under adverse scenarios.

Sector and geographic diversification provide some of the most reliable correlation benefits for equity portfolios. Technology stocks often behave differently from utility stocks, while domestic stocks frequently show different patterns from international holdings. However, these correlation benefits can deteriorate during broad market stress when investors indiscriminately sell all risky assets regardless of their fundamental characteristics.

Fixed-income holdings traditionally provide negative correlation benefits with equity positions, particularly high-quality government bonds that often appreciate when stock markets decline as investors seek safety. However, this relationship can break down during periods of inflation concerns or fiscal uncertainty when both stocks and bonds face pressure from rising interest rates.

Alternative asset classes including commodities, real estate, and hedge fund strategies can provide correlation benefits, though these relationships tend to be unstable and may not persist during the specific market conditions when diversification is most needed. The complexity and costs associated with alternative investments should be weighed against their potential correlation benefits.

Rebalancing disciplines: Systematic approaches to maintain target allocations

Rebalancing represents the systematic process of returning portfolio allocations to target percentages after market movements have caused drift from intended strategic allocation targets. This discipline forces investors to sell portions of assets that have become overweighted and purchase additional amounts of assets that have become underweighted, implementing a systematic buy-low, sell-high approach that can enhance long-term returns while maintaining risk control.

The mathematical foundation of rebalancing benefits stems from volatility drag and the arithmetic of returning to mean allocations. When volatile assets deviate from target allocations and then return to those targets through rebalancing, the selling of appreciated assets and purchasing of depreciated assets can generate returns that exceed simple buy-and-hold strategies, particularly when asset classes show mean-reverting tendencies over time.

However, rebalancing benefits are not guaranteed and depend on specific market conditions and asset class relationships. During sustained trending markets where certain asset classes consistently outperform others, rebalancing can reduce returns by forcing sales of winning assets and purchases of losing assets. The key to successful rebalancing lies in understanding when the benefits are likely to exceed the costs and implementing systems that capture these benefits efficiently.

Threshold-based rebalancing triggers adjustments when allocations drift beyond predetermined tolerance bands around target percentages. For example, an investor with a target sixty percent stock allocation might rebalance when stock holdings exceed sixty-five percent or fall below fifty-five percent of total portfolio value. This approach ensures that portfolios don't drift too far from intended risk levels while avoiding excessive trading during normal market fluctuations.

Time-based rebalancing occurs at predetermined intervals regardless of how much allocations have drifted from targets. Monthly, quarterly, or annual rebalancing schedules provide systematic approaches that can be implemented automatically while reducing the behavioral challenges associated with making discretionary rebalancing decisions during emotional market periods.

Combination approaches use both threshold and time-based triggers to optimize rebalancing effectiveness while managing implementation costs. These systems might rebalance quarterly if allocations have drifted beyond tolerance bands or annually regardless of drift amounts, ensuring that portfolios receive regular maintenance while avoiding excessive trading costs.

Tax considerations significantly impact rebalancing decisions for portfolios held in taxable accounts, as rebalancing sales can generate taxable capital gains that reduce net returns. Tax-efficient rebalancing strategies might prioritize rebalancing within tax-advantaged accounts, use new contributions to restore target allocations, or implement tax-loss harvesting to offset rebalancing gains with losses from other positions.

Cash flow rebalancing uses new contributions and withdrawals to adjust portfolio allocations without triggering taxable events. Rather than selling overweighted positions, new investment flows are directed toward underweighted asset classes until target allocations are restored. This approach works well for investors making regular contributions but may not be sufficient for portfolios experiencing significant allocation drift.

The frequency and methodology of rebalancing should align with individual circumstances, risk tolerance, and portfolio characteristics. More frequent rebalancing provides better risk control but increases transaction costs and tax consequences. Less frequent rebalancing reduces implementation costs but allows greater allocation drift that could expose portfolios to unintended risks.

Behavioral benefits of systematic rebalancing often exceed the mathematical advantages by providing discipline during emotionally challenging market periods. The commitment to predetermined rebalancing rules helps investors maintain long-term strategic focus rather than making impulsive allocation changes based on recent market performance or media commentary.

Implementation of rebalancing disciplines requires establishing clear rules before they are needed and maintaining commitment to these rules during periods when emotions suggest different courses of action. The most successful rebalancing strategies are those that can be implemented systematically without requiring complex judgmental decisions during stressful market conditions.

5.2 Risk Mitigation Strategies

Risk mitigation in portfolio management extends far beyond simple diversification to encompass a comprehensive framework of strategies designed to protect capital while maintaining growth potential. Effective risk management recognizes that different types of risks require different mitigation approaches and that the cost of protection must be balanced against the potential benefits during adverse market conditions.

Position limits and diversification rules: Avoiding concentration risk

Concentration risk represents one of the most common and dangerous threats to long-term investment success, as excessive allocation to any single position, sector, or geographic region can expose portfolios to catastrophic losses that diversification could have prevented. Establishing and maintaining systematic position limits provides the discipline necessary to avoid the overconfidence and familiarity bias that often lead investors to concentrate too heavily in their favorite investments or employers' stocks.

Individual position limits typically range from two to eight percent of total portfolio value, depending on the investor's risk tolerance and the quality of the underlying investment. High-conviction positions in well-understood, high-quality companies might warrant allocations toward the upper end of this range, while speculative investments or companies in volatile industries should be limited to smaller percentages that cannot materially damage overall portfolio performance if they fail completely.

The enforcement of position limits requires systematic monitoring and rebalancing as successful investments grow to represent larger portfolio percentages. Many investors make the mistake of allowing winning positions to grow unchecked, creating dangerous concentrations that expose them to single-stock risk that could have been avoided through disciplined profit-taking and rebalancing.

Sector diversification rules prevent overconcentration in particular industries or business models that might appear attractive during specific market cycles but expose portfolios to systematic risks that affect all companies within those sectors. Technology stocks during the late 1990s and financial stocks during the mid-2000s provide examples of sectors that seemed unstoppable until fundamental changes caused widespread declines that affected even the highest-quality companies within those industries.

Geographic diversification limits extend beyond domestic versus international allocation to consider exposure to specific countries or regions that might face political, economic, or currency risks. Emerging market investments, while potentially offering higher returns, require position limits that reflect their higher volatility and political risks compared to developed market allocations.

Hedging techniques for beginners: Using inverse ETFs and protective puts

Hedging strategies provide insurance against adverse market movements by establishing positions that should increase in value when primary holdings decline, offering protection that can reduce portfolio volatility and preserve capital during market downturns. However, hedging involves costs and complexity that require careful consideration to ensure that protection benefits justify their expense.

Inverse exchange-traded funds offer a relatively simple hedging approach that allows investors to profit from market declines without the complexity of short selling individual stocks. These funds use derivatives and short positions to deliver returns that move opposite to their underlying indices, providing gains when markets decline and losses when markets advance. However, inverse ETFs typically experience tracking error and decay over time that makes them unsuitable for long-term holdings and most effective as short-term hedging tools.

The daily rebalancing mechanism that most inverse ETFs employ causes performance to deviate from expected results over extended periods, particularly during volatile markets where frequent direction changes can erode returns even when the overall market movement aligns with the fund's intended direction. This characteristic makes inverse ETFs most suitable for hedging specific event risks or short-term market concerns rather than permanent portfolio allocations.

Protective put options provide more precise hedging capabilities by granting the right to sell specific stocks or indices at predetermined prices, offering downside protection while maintaining upside participation if markets continue advancing. Put options function like insurance policies that pay off when the protected assets decline below specified levels, providing known maximum loss levels in exchange for premium payments.

The selection of appropriate strike prices and expiration dates requires balancing protection effectiveness with cost considerations. Out-of-the-money puts offer less expensive protection but provide cushions only after portfolios have already experienced significant declines. At-the-money puts offer more complete protection but at higher premium costs that can significantly reduce returns if protection isn't needed.

Scenario analysis and stress testing: Preparing for market downturns

Scenario analysis provides systematic frameworks for evaluating how portfolios might perform during various adverse market conditions, helping investors understand potential risks and adjust allocations before problems occur rather than reacting after losses have already materialized. This forward-looking approach enables proactive risk management that can prevent many of the behavioral mistakes that occur when investors face unexpected losses.

Historical scenario analysis examines how current portfolio allocations would have performed during past market crises, providing concrete examples of potential downside risks under specific conditions. Testing portfolios against periods like the 2008 financial crisis, the 2000-2002 technology crash, or the 1973-1974 bear market reveals vulnerability patterns and potential loss magnitudes that help calibrate risk expectations.

However, historical analysis has limitations because future crises may differ significantly from past events, and the specific combinations of asset classes and geographic exposures in current portfolios may not have existed during historical stress periods. The increasing correlations between global markets and asset classes mean that traditional diversification assumptions may not hold during future crisis periods.

Monte Carlo simulation provides more comprehensive stress testing by generating thousands of potential market scenarios based on statistical properties of asset class returns and correlations. These simulations can reveal the range of possible portfolio outcomes over different time horizons while identifying the probability of achieving specific financial goals or avoiding unacceptable losses.

Stress testing should examine not only portfolio value changes during adverse scenarios but also the behavioral and practical implications of potential losses. A portfolio that declines thirty percent might be mathematically acceptable but emotionally unbearable for investors who haven't prepared psychologically for such losses. Understanding personal loss tolerance helps design portfolios that investors can maintain during difficult periods rather than abandoning strategies at precisely the wrong times.

5.3 Tax-Efficient Portfolio Management

Tax efficiency represents a crucial but often overlooked component of portfolio management that can significantly impact after-tax returns over extended investment periods. The difference between pre-tax and after-tax returns compounds over time, making tax-efficient strategies increasingly valuable for long-term investors. Developing systematic approaches to minimize tax drag while maintaining optimal investment strategies requires understanding the complex interactions between investment decisions and tax consequences.

Tax-loss harvesting tactics: Turning losses into tax savings

Tax-loss harvesting involves systematically realizing investment losses to offset taxable gains from other portfolio positions, reducing current tax obligations while maintaining appropriate investment exposure through replacement securities. This strategy transforms inevitable investment losses into valuable tax deductions that can enhance after-tax returns significantly over time.

The fundamental principle underlying tax-loss harvesting recognizes that investment losses are inevitable in diversified portfolios, but their timing can be controlled to maximize tax benefits. Rather than allowing losses to remain unrealized while gains accumulate tax obligations, systematic harvesting realizes losses strategically to offset gains and reduce overall tax burdens.

Direct tax-loss harvesting involves selling positions that have declined in value and immediately purchasing similar but not identical securities to maintain market exposure while avoiding wash sale rules that would disallow the tax deduction. For example, an investor might sell a large-cap growth fund that has declined and immediately purchase a different large-cap growth fund with similar characteristics but sufficient differences to satisfy tax regulations.

The wash sale rule prevents investors from claiming tax losses on securities that are repurchased within thirty days before or after the sale, requiring careful selection of replacement securities that provide similar exposure without triggering disqualification. This rule applies not only to identical securities but also to substantially identical securities, making it important to understand which investments are considered too similar for effective tax-loss harvesting.

Systematic tax-loss harvesting requires ongoing monitoring of portfolio positions to identify opportunities for beneficial trades while avoiding excessive turnover that could generate high transaction costs. Many investors implement threshold-based systems that trigger harvesting when losses exceed specific dollar amounts or percentages, ensuring that harvesting activities focus on meaningful opportunities rather than small losses that don't justify transaction costs.

The coordination of tax-loss harvesting with rebalancing activities can enhance efficiency by accomplishing multiple portfolio management objectives through single transactions. When rebalancing requires reducing overweighted positions that happen to show losses, these sales can serve both rebalancing and tax-loss harvesting purposes simultaneously.

Asset location optimization: Which investments belong in which accounts

Asset location optimization involves strategically placing different types of investments in taxable versus tax-advantaged accounts to minimize overall tax obligations while maintaining desired portfolio allocations across all account types. This strategy recognizes that different account types offer different tax treatment and that careful placement of assets can significantly enhance after-tax returns.

Tax-inefficient investments that generate significant amounts of taxable income or short-term capital gains typically belong in tax-deferred accounts like traditional IRAs and 401k plans where these tax consequences can be avoided until withdrawal. Real estate investment trusts, high-yield bonds, and actively managed funds that generate frequent distributions often prove more tax-efficient when held in retirement accounts rather than taxable accounts.

Tax-efficient investments that generate primarily long-term capital gains or qualified dividends may be better suited for taxable accounts where these favorable tax treatments can be utilized. Index funds, individual stocks held for long periods, and municipal bonds often work well in taxable accounts where their tax-efficient characteristics provide maximum benefits.

Growth-oriented investments that are expected to appreciate significantly over long periods often belong in Roth IRA accounts where future appreciation can be harvested tax-free rather than being subject to ordinary income tax rates when withdrawn from traditional retirement accounts. This strategy proves most valuable for younger investors with long time horizons who can maximize the tax-free compounding benefits of Roth accounts.

International investments present particular asset location considerations due to foreign tax credit opportunities that are only available in taxable accounts. International funds held in tax-deferred accounts cannot pass through foreign tax credits to investors, potentially making taxable account placement more beneficial despite the generally tax-inefficient nature of international fund distributions.

Long-term vs. short-term planning: Minimizing tax drag on returns

Tax-efficient investing requires balancing short-term tax minimization with long-term wealth accumulation goals, recognizing that strategies that minimize current taxes may not always optimize after-tax wealth over extended periods. Developing comprehensive approaches that consider both current and future tax implications enables more effective overall tax management.

Long-term capital gains treatment provides one of the most valuable tax advantages available to individual investors, offering significantly lower tax rates for investments held more than one year compared to ordinary income tax rates applied to short-term gains. This preferential treatment creates powerful incentives for patient investing approaches that emphasize long holding periods over frequent trading strategies.

The holding period requirement for long-term capital gains treatment encourages investment strategies that align with fundamental analysis and business ownership mentalities rather than short-term trading approaches. This alignment between tax efficiency and sound investment practices represents one of the few areas where tax considerations support rather than complicate optimal investment decision-making.

Tax-deferred account contributions provide immediate tax deductions while deferring taxes until retirement when tax rates may be lower due to reduced income levels. However, this strategy requires careful consideration of current versus future tax rate expectations and the trade-offs between immediate deductions and tax-free Roth account growth.

Estate planning considerations become increasingly important for larger portfolios where tax-efficient wealth transfer strategies can significantly impact after-tax legacy values. Gifting appreciated securities, establishing charitable trusts, and utilizing other estate planning techniques can reduce overall tax burdens while supporting philanthropic objectives and family wealth transfer goals.

The integration of tax planning with investment strategy requires ongoing attention as tax laws change and personal circumstances evolve over time. Regular reviews of asset location strategies, tax-loss harvesting opportunities, and long-term tax planning approaches ensure that portfolios remain optimized for current regulations and individual situations.

Chapter 6: Global Investing and Currency Dynamics

International stocks represent forty-four percent of global market capitalization, yet American investors allocate only fifteen percent of their portfolios to international markets, effectively missing half the world's investment opportunities. This home bias represents one of the most significant strategic mistakes in modern portfolio construction, depriving investors of diversification benefits, growth opportunities, and risk-adjusted returns that global investing can provide. Understanding how to access international markets efficiently while managing the associated risks and complexities represents a crucial skill for sophisticated investors seeking to optimize their long-term wealth creation potential.

6.1 International Market Access

Accessing international investment opportunities requires understanding the various mechanisms available to American investors, each with distinct advantages, limitations, and cost structures that can significantly impact investment outcomes. The evolution of global financial markets has created multiple pathways for international investing, ranging from simple domestic instruments that provide foreign exposure to direct investment in foreign securities that offer more comprehensive access but greater complexity.

The choice of international investment approach depends on numerous factors including investment objectives, portfolio size, tax considerations, currency preferences, and comfort level with foreign market complexity. Sophisticated investors often employ multiple approaches simultaneously to optimize their international exposure while managing costs and risks that accompany global investing.

ADRs vs. direct foreign investment: Pros, cons, and tax implications

American Depositary Receipts represent the most accessible method for U.S. investors to own foreign stocks while maintaining the convenience and regulatory protections of domestic securities trading. These instruments are created when foreign shares are deposited with American depositary banks, which then issue receipts representing ownership of the underlying foreign securities that trade on U.S. exchanges like domestic stocks.

The structure of ADR programs provides several significant advantages for American investors seeking international exposure. Trading occurs during U.S. market hours using dollar pricing, eliminating the complexity of foreign exchange transactions and time zone coordination required for direct foreign investment. Settlement occurs through standard U.S. clearing systems, reducing operational risk and providing familiar trade confirmation and reporting procedures that match domestic investment processes.

Regulatory oversight of ADR programs provides additional investor protections through SEC registration requirements that mandate financial reporting in accordance with U.S. generally accepted accounting principles or comprehensive reconciliations that help American investors understand foreign company financial statements. This regulatory framework reduces some of the information risk associated with foreign investing while providing legal recourse mechanisms familiar to U.S. investors.

However, ADR investing involves several limitations and costs that can impact investment performance and strategic flexibility. The ADR structure typically involves fees charged by depositary banks for various services including dividend processing, annual maintenance, and corporate action handling that can reduce effective returns compared to direct foreign investment. These fees often range from one to three cents per share annually plus transaction-based charges that can accumulate significantly over time.

The universe of companies available through ADR programs represents only a fraction of international investment opportunities, with coverage heavily weighted toward larger, more established companies that meet ADR program requirements. This selection bias can limit access to smaller companies, emerging market opportunities, or specialized sectors that might offer superior growth prospects but don't justify ADR program establishment costs.

Currency hedging considerations add complexity to ADR analysis, as different ADR programs employ varying approaches to currency exposure that can significantly impact returns for U.S. dollar-based investors. Some ADRs provide natural currency hedging through their underlying business operations, while others maintain full foreign currency exposure that can create additional volatility and return uncertainty.

Direct foreign investment provides more comprehensive access to international markets through brokerage platforms that enable trading in foreign securities on their home exchanges. This approach offers broader investment universes including smaller companies, specialized sectors, and markets that lack substantial ADR representation, potentially providing superior diversification and return opportunities.

The operational complexity of direct foreign investment requires understanding settlement procedures, custody arrangements, and regulatory requirements that vary significantly across different markets. European markets typically provide relatively straightforward access for American investors, while Asian and emerging markets often involve additional documentation, minimum investment requirements, or restricted access that can complicate investment implementation.

Tax implications of direct foreign investment can be significantly more complex than ADR investing, particularly regarding foreign tax credits, treaty benefits, and reporting requirements that may require professional tax advice to optimize. Different countries impose varying withholding tax rates on dividends and capital gains that can impact after-tax returns, though tax treaties often provide mechanisms to reduce these burdens for qualifying investors.

Emerging vs. developed markets: Risk-reward profiles and entry strategies

The distinction between developed and emerging markets represents one of the most important strategic decisions in international investing, as these market categories exhibit fundamentally different risk-reward characteristics that require distinct analytical approaches and portfolio management techniques. Understanding these differences enables more informed allocation decisions and appropriate risk management for international portfolio components.

Developed markets typically include countries with mature economies, stable political systems, established financial markets, and strong regulatory frameworks that provide relatively predictable investment environments. These markets generally offer lower expected returns than emerging markets but with correspondingly lower volatility and political risk that can provide portfolio stability and diversification benefits relative to domestic U.S. investments.

The infrastructure quality of developed markets typically provides superior liquidity, efficient price discovery, and reliable settlement systems that reduce operational risk and enable larger position sizes without significant market impact. Professional analyst coverage and financial reporting standards in developed markets often provide more comprehensive information for investment decision-making, though this transparency can also result in more efficient pricing that reduces opportunities for superior returns through fundamental analysis.

Currency stability in developed markets generally provides more predictable foreign exchange risk profiles, though currency movements can still significantly impact returns for dollar-based investors. Major developed market currencies like the euro, yen, and pound sterling typically exhibit lower volatility than emerging market currencies while maintaining sufficient liquidity for effective hedging strategies when desired.

Emerging markets encompass countries with developing economies that offer higher expected returns but with significantly higher volatility, political risk, and operational complexity that require careful risk management and thorough due diligence. These markets often benefit from favorable demographic trends, rapid economic growth, and increasing integration into global economic systems that can provide superior long-term investment opportunities for patient investors.

The growth potential of emerging markets stems from multiple factors including younger populations entering peak economic productivity, urbanization trends that concentrate economic activity, and technological adoption that can accelerate economic development. These structural trends can create multi-decade investment opportunities that developed markets may not offer due to their economic maturity and demographic challenges.

However, emerging market investing requires sophisticated understanding of political risk, regulatory uncertainty, and currency volatility that can overwhelm the fundamental return potential of underlying investments. Political instability, policy changes, and international relations can create dramatic short-term volatility that tests investor patience and risk tolerance while potentially offering attractive long-term opportunities for disciplined investors.

Market structure considerations in emerging markets often involve lower liquidity, less efficient price discovery, and potentially unreliable settlement systems that increase operational risk and may limit position sizing for larger portfolios. Professional analyst coverage may be limited or less reliable than in developed markets, requiring more intensive fundamental research and due diligence to identify attractive investment opportunities.

Country-specific ETFs and funds: Gaining targeted international exposure

Exchange-traded funds and mutual funds focused on specific countries or regions provide systematic approaches to international investing that can offer broad market exposure while eliminating the complexity of individual security selection in foreign markets. These vehicles enable targeted geographic allocation strategies while providing professional management and diversification that individual investors might find difficult to achieve through direct investment approaches.

Country-specific ETFs typically track broad market indices within targeted countries, providing exposure to the largest and most liquid companies in those markets while maintaining cost structures significantly lower than actively managed alternatives. These funds offer precise geographic targeting that enables tactical allocation strategies based on economic, political, or valuation considerations specific to individual countries or regions.

The index construction methodology of country ETFs significantly impacts their investment characteristics, with some funds using market capitalization weighting that can create concentration in the largest companies while others employ alternative weighting schemes designed to provide more balanced exposure across different company sizes or sectors. Understanding these methodological differences helps investors select funds that align with their specific exposure objectives.

Sector concentration represents a crucial consideration when evaluating country-specific funds, as some national markets exhibit heavy weightings in particular industries that can create unintended sector bets rather than pure geographic diversification. For example, technology-heavy markets might provide sector exposure that overlaps significantly with domestic technology holdings, while commodity-dependent markets might create energy or materials concentration that differs from intended geographic diversification.

Regional funds provide broader geographic diversification within specific areas like Europe, Asia-Pacific, or Latin America while maintaining more targeted exposure than global international funds. These vehicles can offer attractive middle ground approaches that provide geographic diversification while maintaining some ability to make regional allocation decisions based on economic or political developments.

Actively managed international funds provide professional security selection and risk management that can potentially add value through superior stock selection, country allocation, and currency management. However, these benefits come with higher cost structures and potential for underperformance that requires careful evaluation of management track records and investment processes.

The tax efficiency of different international fund structures can significantly impact after-tax returns, with ETFs typically providing superior tax characteristics compared to mutual funds due to their in-kind redemption mechanisms that can minimize taxable distributions. However, foreign tax credits and treaty benefits may be passed through more effectively by certain fund structures, requiring analysis of total tax impact rather than simply comparing expense ratios.

Currency hedging options within international funds provide different approaches to foreign exchange risk management, with some funds offering currency-hedged variants that attempt to eliminate currency volatility while others maintain full currency exposure. The decision between hedged and unhedged international exposure depends on individual risk tolerance and views about currency diversification benefits versus volatility reduction through hedging.

Liquidity considerations become particularly important for country-specific funds focusing on smaller or less developed markets, as underlying market liquidity constraints can impact fund performance during periods of significant redemptions or subscriptions. Understanding the daily trading volumes and bid-ask spreads of these funds helps ensure they can be efficiently traded without significant market impact costs that could erode investment returns.

6.2 Currency Risk and Opportunity

Currency fluctuations represent both the greatest risk and most significant opportunity in international investing, as foreign exchange movements can overwhelm the fundamental performance of underlying investments while simultaneously creating profit opportunities for investors who understand and can navigate currency dynamics effectively. The relationship between currency movements and international investment returns requires sophisticated analysis that goes beyond simple hedging decisions to encompass strategic positioning based on macroeconomic trends, central bank policies, and long-term purchasing power relationships.

Hedging foreign exchange exposure: When and how to protect returns

Currency hedging represents a systematic approach to reducing or eliminating foreign exchange risk in international portfolios, providing protection against adverse currency movements while potentially sacrificing beneficial currency effects that could enhance returns. The decision to hedge currency exposure requires careful analysis of costs, benefits, and strategic objectives that vary significantly based on investment timeframes, risk tolerance, and views about currency market efficiency.

The fundamental principle underlying currency hedging recognizes that foreign investments involve two distinct sources of return: the performance of underlying assets denominated in local currencies and the movement of those currencies relative to the investor's home currency. These two return components can move independently and sometimes in opposite directions, creating situations where excellent underlying asset performance gets overwhelmed by adverse currency movements or poor asset performance gets masked by favorable exchange rate changes.

Perfect currency hedging theoretically eliminates foreign exchange risk by establishing offsetting positions that neutralize currency movements, allowing investors to capture pure local market returns without currency impact. However, perfect hedging involves costs and complexity that may not be justified for all international investments, particularly when currency movements provide natural diversification benefits that reduce overall portfolio volatility.

The cost-benefit analysis of currency hedging requires understanding both explicit costs like forward contract premiums or options premiums and implicit costs including tracking error, operational complexity, and opportunity costs of foregone favorable currency movements. Forward contracts typically provide the most cost-effective hedging mechanism for large positions but require precise sizing and active management to maintain hedge effectiveness as portfolio values and currency levels change over time.

Currency hedging effectiveness depends heavily on the correlation between underlying asset performance and currency movements, with hedging providing the greatest benefit when these factors move independently and the least benefit when they move together. Commodity-exporting countries often show positive correlation between currency strength and equity market performance, reducing the diversification benefits of hedging while potentially increasing portfolio volatility when both currency and equity hedges move against the investor simultaneously.

Dynamic hedging strategies attempt to optimize hedge ratios based on changing market conditions, risk levels, and correlation patterns rather than maintaining fixed hedge percentages regardless of circumstances. These approaches might increase hedging during periods of high currency volatility while reducing hedges when currency trends align favorably with portfolio objectives, though dynamic strategies require sophisticated analysis and active management that might not be appropriate for all investors.

The time horizon for international investments significantly influences optimal hedging decisions, with shorter investment periods typically warranting higher hedge ratios due to the greater potential for currency volatility to dominate investment outcomes over brief periods. Longer investment horizons often reduce the need for extensive hedging as currency movements tend to exhibit mean-reverting characteristics that reduce their impact on long-term returns.

Currency trend exploitation: Profiting from dollar cycles

Currency markets exhibit persistent trending behavior that sophisticated investors can potentially exploit through systematic analysis of fundamental factors that drive long-term exchange rate movements. The U.S. dollar's unique position as the world's primary reserve currency creates cyclical patterns in dollar strength that influence global capital flows, commodity prices, and international investment opportunities in predictable ways that can guide strategic positioning decisions.

Dollar strength cycles typically begin during periods of relative U.S. economic strength, rising interest rates, or global uncertainty that drives international investors toward dollar-denominated safe haven assets. These cycles can persist for multiple years and create systematic headwinds for international investments while potentially providing opportunities in dollar-denominated assets or sectors that benefit from strong dollar conditions.

The impact of dollar strength extends beyond simple translation effects to influence the fundamental performance of international companies through trade competitiveness, input costs, and financing conditions that can create multi-year investment themes. Companies with significant dollar-denominated revenues often outperform during strong dollar periods even when their local currencies weaken, while companies with dollar-denominated costs and local currency revenues typically underperform during these cycles.

Conversely, dollar weakness cycles often coincide with international outperformance as foreign currencies appreciate against the dollar while international economic growth accelerates relative to U.S. conditions. These cycles can provide multi-year tailwinds for international investments while creating challenges for domestic companies that compete internationally or rely on international markets for growth.

The predictability of dollar cycles stems from fundamental factors including interest rate differentials, economic growth comparisons, current account balances, and political stability measures that influence international capital flows and currency demand. Central bank policy coordination and intervention activities can accelerate or moderate these cycles but rarely reverse fundamental trends that persist until underlying economic imbalances correct.

Commodity price relationships provide additional insights into dollar cycle analysis, as commodities typically exhibit inverse correlations with dollar strength that reflect both currency effects and global demand patterns. Strong dollar periods often coincide with commodity price weakness that can create opportunities in resource-rich countries or commodity-dependent economies while challenging countries that depend on commodity imports.

Purchasing power parity plays: Finding currency-driven mispricings

Purchasing power parity theory provides a fundamental framework for identifying currency mispricings by comparing the relative costs of goods and services across different countries to determine whether exchange rates accurately reflect underlying economic values. While PPP relationships rarely hold precisely in the short term, significant deviations from PPP often indicate currency mispricings that can create attractive investment opportunities for patient investors willing to wait for eventual corrections.

The application of PPP analysis requires understanding different methodologies for measuring price levels and their appropriate applications for investment decision-making. The Big Mac Index, popularized by The Economist, provides a simplified but practical approach to PPP analysis by comparing the local currency prices of McDonald's Big Mac sandwiches across different countries to identify potentially undervalued or overvalued currencies.

More sophisticated PPP analysis incorporates broader price surveys that include housing costs, services, and tradable goods while adjusting for quality differences and consumption patterns that vary across countries. The Penn World Table and similar academic resources provide comprehensive PPP data that can guide long-term currency and international investment decisions, though these measures often differ significantly from financial market exchange rates due to capital flows and speculative activity that can persist for extended periods.

The investment applications of PPP analysis extend beyond pure currency speculation to encompass international stock selection based on currency-adjusted valuations that can reveal mispricings created by exchange rate distortions. Companies operating in countries with undervalued currencies might appear expensive based on dollar-converted metrics while actually trading at reasonable valuations when adjusted for PPP relationships, creating opportunities for investors who can look beyond surface-level currency translations.

Real estate investment trusts and property-focused companies often provide attractive PPP-based opportunities because real estate values typically exhibit stronger relationships with local purchasing power than internationally traded goods or services. Countries with currencies significantly undervalued relative to PPP often offer real estate investments that provide both currency appreciation potential and attractive local market fundamentals.

The timing of PPP-based investments requires patience and strong conviction, as currency mispricings can persist for years or even decades before eventually correcting toward fundamental values. The carry trade phenomenon, where investors borrow low-yielding currencies to invest in high-yielding alternatives, can perpetuate currency mispricings while providing income that partially offsets the waiting period required for PPP convergence.

6.3 Geopolitical Risk Assessment

Geopolitical risks represent some of the most challenging yet potentially rewarding aspects of international investing, as political developments, policy changes, and international relations can create dramatic short-term volatility while generating long-term opportunities for investors who can accurately assess and navigate political complexity. Understanding geopolitical risk requires systematic frameworks for evaluating political stability, policy direction, and international relationships that influence investment outcomes in ways that traditional financial analysis cannot capture.

Political risk frameworks: Evaluating stability and policy directions

Political risk assessment requires comprehensive frameworks that can evaluate multiple dimensions of political stability and policy predictability while recognizing that different types of political risks affect different investments in varying ways. Systematic political analysis helps investors distinguish between temporary political noise that creates short-term volatility and fundamental political changes that could permanently alter investment landscapes.

Institutional quality assessment forms the foundation of political risk analysis by evaluating the strength, transparency, and predictability of political institutions including legal systems, regulatory agencies, and democratic processes that provide frameworks for business operations and investment protection. Countries with strong institutional frameworks typically provide more predictable investment environments even when experiencing political transitions, while weak institutional environments create heightened uncertainty regardless of current political leadership.

The measurement of institutional quality incorporates factors including rule of law effectiveness, regulatory transparency, corruption levels, and property rights protection that directly impact business operations and investment returns. International organizations including the World Bank, Transparency International, and Freedom House provide systematic institutional quality measurements that enable comparative analysis across countries and historical tracking of institutional improvements or deterioration.

Policy continuity analysis examines the likelihood that current economic and regulatory policies will persist through political transitions, helping investors understand whether political changes might disrupt favorable business environments or investment frameworks. Countries with strong policy institutions and broad political consensus around economic policies typically maintain greater policy continuity than those with polarized political systems or weak institutional frameworks.

Electoral cycle considerations add temporal dimensions to political risk assessment, as upcoming elections can create policy uncertainty while election outcomes might dramatically alter regulatory environments or international relationships. Understanding electoral dynamics, candidate policy positions, and likely coalition outcomes helps investors anticipate potential policy changes and position portfolios appropriately for different political scenarios.

Social stability indicators including income inequality measures, demographic trends, and social cohesion metrics provide context for understanding political sustainability and the likelihood of social unrest that could disrupt business operations or trigger policy responses. Countries experiencing rapid demographic changes or increasing inequality often face greater political pressures that could result in policy changes affecting business environments or investment frameworks.

Trade flow analysis: Understanding global supply chain investments

Global trade relationships create complex interdependencies that influence investment opportunities and risks across multiple countries and industries, requiring sophisticated analysis of trade flows, supply chain structures, and policy relationships that determine competitive advantages and vulnerability patterns. Understanding these trade dynamics enables more informed investment decisions while revealing opportunities and risks that purely domestic analysis might miss.

Bilateral trade relationship analysis examines the economic interdependencies between specific countries that create both opportunities and vulnerabilities for companies operating across these relationships. Countries with complementary trade relationships often provide more stable investment environments than those with competitive or adversarial trade positions, though excessive dependence on single trade partners can create concentration risks that policy changes or economic disruptions could exploit.

Supply chain mapping reveals how global production networks distribute economic value and risk across different countries and regions, helping investors understand which locations provide critical supply chain functions versus those that serve primarily as final assembly or distribution points. Companies controlling critical supply chain chokepoints often possess sustainable competitive advantages, while those operating in easily replaceable supply chain segments face greater competitive pressures and profit margin compression.

The analysis of supply chain resilience has become increasingly important following recent disruptions including the COVID-19 pandemic, trade wars, and geopolitical conflicts that revealed vulnerabilities in globally integrated production systems. Companies and countries that can provide supply chain alternatives or domestic production capabilities often benefit during supply chain disruption periods while those dependent on vulnerable supply chains face operational and financial stress.

Trade policy impact assessment requires understanding how different trade agreements, tariff structures, and regulatory frameworks influence competitive dynamics and profitability across different industries and geographic regions. Changes in trade policies can dramatically alter competitive landscapes by shifting cost structures, market access conditions, or regulatory requirements that affect business profitability and investment attractiveness.

Commodity trade flow analysis provides insights into resource dependencies and export opportunities that influence currency movements, economic growth patterns, and investment opportunities across resource-rich and resource-poor countries.

Understanding these commodity interdependencies helps investors anticipate how commodity price changes might affect different countries and investment opportunities while identifying potential supply security issues that could create investment themes.

Regulatory arbitrage opportunities: Profiting from different market rules

Regulatory differences across international markets create arbitrage opportunities for sophisticated investors who can identify situations where identical or similar assets trade at different valuations due to regulatory constraints, market access limitations, or legal structures that create artificial price differences. These opportunities require deep understanding of regulatory frameworks and their practical implications for market efficiency and pricing mechanisms.

Cross-listing arbitrage opportunities emerge when companies trade on multiple exchanges under different regulatory frameworks that create price discrepancies between identical securities trading in different markets. These arbitrages often reflect differences in investor access, regulatory requirements, or currency effects that create temporary pricing inefficiencies sophisticated investors can exploit through simultaneous buying and selling across different markets.

Tax regime optimization involves structuring international investments to minimize tax obligations through legitimate use of different countries' tax treaties, withholding tax rates, and legal structures that can significantly enhance after-tax returns. Understanding international tax planning requires professional expertise but can provide substantial return enhancement opportunities, particularly for larger portfolios that can justify the complexity and professional costs involved.

Regulatory environment comparisons reveal how different countries' regulatory approaches create competitive advantages or disadvantages for specific industries or business models, creating investment opportunities in countries with favorable regulatory frameworks while avoiding those with restrictive approaches. Financial services, technology, healthcare, and energy industries often show significant performance differences based on regulatory environments that support or constrain business development.

Market structure arbitrage opportunities arise from differences in market organization, trading mechanisms, and participant access that can create pricing inefficiencies between similar markets or securities. Understanding these structural differences enables more effective execution of international investment strategies while potentially identifying pure arbitrage opportunities that provide risk-free profits through simultaneous transactions across different market structures.

The sustainability of regulatory arbitrage opportunities depends on the likelihood that regulatory differences will persist versus converge over time through international coordination or competitive pressure. Some regulatory differences represent fundamental philosophical approaches that are likely to persist, while others might reflect temporary policy positions that could change as governments respond to competitive pressures or international coordination efforts.

Chapter 7: Advanced Strategies and Future Trends

Artificial intelligence now manages over four trillion dollars in assets, blockchain technology is revolutionizing trade settlement, and retail investors possess more analytical power and market access than ever before in financial history. The convergence of technological advancement, regulatory evolution, and democratized information access is fundamentally transforming the investment landscape in ways that will reshape portfolio management, risk assessment, and return generation for decades to come. Understanding these technological shifts and their practical applications represents a crucial advantage for investors seeking to maintain competitiveness in an increasingly sophisticated and algorithm-driven marketplace.

7.1 Technology-Driven Investing

The integration of advanced technology into investment processes represents one of the most significant developments in modern finance, creating opportunities for individual investors to access institutional-quality analytical tools while simultaneously requiring new skills and understanding to navigate increasingly complex technological landscapes. Technology-driven investing encompasses a broad spectrum of approaches from automated portfolio management and alternative data analysis to sophisticated quantitative strategies that were previously available only to well-funded institutional investors.

The democratization of investment technology has fundamentally altered the competitive landscape by providing individual investors with access to computational power, data sources, and analytical frameworks that rival those used by professional money managers. This technological leveling effect creates both opportunities for superior returns through skillful technology adoption and risks for investors who fail to adapt to increasingly sophisticated market conditions where human intuition alone may prove insufficient.

Robo-advisor integration: Combining human judgment with algorithmic efficiency

Robo-advisor technology represents a sophisticated evolution in portfolio management that combines the consistency and efficiency of algorithmic decision-making with the flexibility to incorporate human judgment and customization that purely automated systems cannot provide. The most effective approaches to robo-advisor integration recognize that different aspects of portfolio management benefit from different combinations of human and algorithmic input, creating hybrid systems that leverage the strengths of both approaches while mitigating their respective weaknesses.

The core competencies of robo-advisor systems include systematic rebalancing, tax-loss harvesting, and asset allocation optimization based on modern portfolio theory principles that benefit from consistent, emotion-free execution that human managers often struggle to maintain during volatile market periods. These systems excel at processing large amounts of market data, maintaining precise target allocations, and implementing rule-based strategies without the behavioral biases that frequently undermine human decision-making during stressful market conditions.

However, robo-advisor limitations become apparent in areas requiring subjective judgment, complex analysis of unique situations, or adaptation to changing circumstances that weren't anticipated in original programming. Market regime changes, geopolitical developments, or individual life changes often require human analysis and decision-making that algorithmic systems cannot adequately address without specific programming updates that might lag behind rapidly evolving conditions.

The integration of human judgment with robo-advisor efficiency typically works best when human input focuses on strategic decisions including goal setting, risk tolerance calibration, and major allocation changes while algorithmic systems handle tactical implementation including rebalancing, tax optimization, and routine maintenance activities. This division of responsibility allows humans to concentrate on areas where judgment and experience add the most value while ensuring consistent execution of routine portfolio management tasks.

Advanced robo-advisor integration might incorporate machine learning algorithms that can adapt their strategies based on changing market conditions or individual investor behavior patterns, though these systems require careful oversight to ensure that algorithmic adaptations align with investor objectives and risk tolerance. The complexity of these adaptive systems creates both opportunities for superior performance and risks of unexpected behavior that human oversight must monitor and manage.

The customization capabilities of hybrid robo-advisor systems enable accommodation of individual preferences, constraints, and objectives that purely standardized algorithmic approaches cannot address effectively. These might include ethical investing constraints, tax situation optimization, or specific risk management requirements that require human input to translate into algorithmic implementation rules that maintain the efficiency benefits of automated execution.

Cost considerations play a crucial role in robo-advisor integration decisions, as the combination of human advisory services with algorithmic implementation typically costs more than purely automated solutions while potentially providing better outcomes that justify the additional expense. Understanding the cost-benefit trade-offs helps investors determine the appropriate level of human-algorithm integration based on portfolio size, complexity, and individual preferences.

Alternative data sources: Satellite imagery, web scraping, and social sentiment

Alternative data represents one of the most rapidly expanding frontiers in investment analysis, providing insights into economic activity, consumer behavior, and business performance that traditional financial statements and economic reports cannot capture in real-time. The proliferation of alternative data sources creates opportunities for individual investors to gain informational advantages that were previously available only to sophisticated institutional investors with substantial technology budgets.

Satellite imagery analysis has emerged as a powerful tool for tracking economic activity, agricultural production, and retail performance through objective measurement of physical activity that precedes traditional economic reporting by weeks or months. Commercial satellite services now provide regular imaging of retail parking lots, manufacturing facilities, agricultural regions, and shipping ports that can reveal business trends and economic patterns before they appear in corporate earnings reports or government statistics.

The application of satellite imagery to investment analysis requires understanding both the technical capabilities and limitations of different imaging technologies while developing analytical frameworks that can translate physical observations into actionable investment insights. Retail investors might use satellite data to track store traffic, construction activity, or inventory levels at major retailers before quarterly earnings announcements, while industrial investors might monitor manufacturing capacity utilization or shipping volumes that indicate business trends.

Web scraping technology enables systematic collection and analysis of vast amounts of publicly available information from corporate websites, job postings, product reviews, and news sources that can provide early indicators of business performance changes. This approach allows investors to track hiring trends, product launch activities, customer satisfaction patterns, or competitive dynamics in real-time rather than waiting for periodic corporate disclosures or analyst reports.

The implementation of web scraping strategies requires technical expertise to design data collection systems while ensuring compliance with website terms of service and legal requirements that govern automated data collection activities. Successful web scraping also requires analytical frameworks that can process large volumes of unstructured data to identify meaningful patterns and trends that translate into actionable investment insights.

Social sentiment analysis leverages natural language processing and machine learning algorithms to analyze social media content, news articles, and online discussions for insights into public opinion, brand perception, and market sentiment that might influence stock prices or business performance. These techniques can identify emerging trends, crisis situations, or shift in consumer preferences before they become apparent through traditional analytical approaches.

The effectiveness of social sentiment analysis depends heavily on the quality of data sources, analytical algorithms, and interpretation frameworks that can distinguish between meaningful sentiment shifts and random noise that characterizes much online discussion. Successful sentiment analysis typically requires combining multiple data sources and analytical approaches to develop robust signals that can guide investment decisions rather than relying on any single sentiment indicator.

Credit card transaction data, when properly aggregated and anonymized, provides real-time insights into consumer spending patterns, retail performance, and economic trends that can help investors anticipate earnings surprises or identify changing competitive dynamics within consumer-focused industries. This data often provides several weeks or months of advance notice compared to traditional earnings reports, creating opportunities for investors who can access and analyze transaction data effectively.

Quantitative strategies for individuals: Building and backtesting systematic approaches

Quantitative investing strategies enable individual investors to develop systematic approaches to security selection, portfolio construction, and risk management based on historical data analysis and mathematical models rather than subjective judgment or fundamental analysis. The democratization of computing power and financial data access has made sophisticated quantitative techniques accessible to individual investors willing to develop the technical skills necessary to implement these approaches effectively.

The foundation of quantitative strategy development begins with identifying and testing investment hypotheses using historical data to determine whether specific factors, patterns, or relationships have provided consistent returns over extended periods. This process requires access to comprehensive historical databases, statistical analysis software, and backtesting platforms that can simulate how different strategies would have performed under various market conditions.

Factor-based investing represents one of the most accessible quantitative approaches for individual investors, involving systematic exposure to specific risk factors including value, momentum, quality, profitability, or low volatility that academic research has identified as sources of excess returns over time. Individual investors can implement factor strategies through focused stock selection, ETF allocation, or custom portfolio construction that emphasizes securities with favorable factor characteristics.

The construction of effective factor strategies requires understanding the academic literature supporting different factors while recognizing that factor performance varies significantly across different market conditions and time periods. Successful factor investing typically involves combining multiple factors that complement each other while avoiding excessive concentration in any single factor that might experience extended periods of underperformance.

Mean reversion strategies attempt to profit from the tendency of security prices to return toward their long-term averages after periods of extreme performance, requiring systematic identification of overbought or oversold conditions that create high-probability reversal opportunities. These strategies work best in range-bound markets but can suffer significant losses during strong trending periods when prices continue moving away from historical averages.

Momentum strategies take the opposite approach by seeking to profit from the tendency of security prices to continue moving in their established directions, requiring systematic identification of trending conditions and appropriate entry and exit criteria that can capture trend continuation while avoiding whipsaw losses when trends reverse. Momentum strategies typically work best during trending market conditions but struggle during choppy, range-bound periods.

Pairs trading strategies attempt to profit from temporary price relationships between related securities by simultaneously buying underperforming securities and selling outperforming ones within pairs that historically move together. These market-neutral approaches can potentially generate returns regardless of overall market direction while requiring sophisticated analysis of correlation relationships and careful risk management to avoid losses when historical relationships break down.

The backtesting process for quantitative strategies requires careful attention to potential biases including survivorship bias, look-ahead bias, and overfitting that can create misleadingly attractive historical performance that doesn't translate into future returns. Proper backtesting involves out-of-sample testing, transaction cost assumptions, and realistic implementation constraints that provide more accurate estimates of strategy effectiveness under real-world conditions.

Risk management becomes particularly crucial for quantitative strategies as systematic approaches can experience rapid losses when market conditions change unexpectedly or when underlying assumptions prove incorrect. Effective quantitative risk management typically involves position limits, stop-loss rules, and portfolio diversification that can limit downside risk while preserving the systematic advantages that quantitative approaches can provide.

The implementation of quantitative strategies requires ongoing monitoring and maintenance to ensure that strategies continue performing as expected while adapting to changing market conditions that might require parameter adjustments or strategy modifications. Successful quantitative investing combines systematic discipline with flexibility to evolve strategies based on changing market dynamics and performance feedback.

Technology platforms for individual quantitative investing continue expanding in capabilities and accessibility, with services like QuantConnect, Zipline, and various brokerage API platforms providing the infrastructure necessary for strategy development, backtesting, and automated execution that were previously available only to institutional investors with substantial technology resources.

7.2 ESG and Impact Investing

Environmental, Social, and Governance investing has evolved from a niche approach focused primarily on avoiding controversial industries to a sophisticated investment framework that seeks to identify companies positioned to thrive in a world increasingly focused on sustainability, social responsibility, and stakeholder capitalism. The integration of ESG factors into investment analysis recognizes that traditional financial metrics may not capture all the risks and opportunities that companies face in an evolving regulatory, social, and environmental landscape where stakeholder expectations extend beyond pure profit maximization.

The growth of ESG investing reflects fundamental shifts in how society evaluates corporate success, with increasing emphasis on long-term value creation that considers environmental impact, social responsibility, and governance quality alongside financial performance. This evolution has created both opportunities for investors who can effectively integrate ESG analysis into their investment processes and challenges in distinguishing between genuine ESG improvements and superficial marketing efforts designed to capture ESG-focused investment flows without underlying business changes.

ESG score interpretation: What ratings really mean for returns

ESG scoring systems attempt to quantify companies' environmental, social, and governance performance through standardized metrics that enable comparison across different companies, industries, and time periods. However, the interpretation of ESG scores requires understanding the methodologies, data sources, and limitations that characterize different rating systems, as these factors significantly influence the meaning and investment relevance of specific scores.

The major ESG rating providers including MSCI, Sustainalytics, and Refinitiv employ different methodologies that can result in dramatically different scores for identical companies, reflecting variations in weighting schemes, data sources, and analytical frameworks that emphasize different aspects of ESG performance. These methodological differences mean that high ESG scores from one provider don't guarantee similar ratings from other providers, making it crucial for investors to understand the specific factors driving scores from their chosen rating system.

Environmental scoring typically focuses on companies' carbon emissions, resource usage, waste management, and exposure to environmental risks including climate change, water scarcity, and regulatory changes related to environmental protection. However, environmental scores often reflect disclosure quality rather than actual environmental performance, as companies with sophisticated sustainability reporting might receive higher scores than those with better actual environmental outcomes but less comprehensive disclosure practices.

The investment implications of environmental scores depend heavily on industry context and regulatory environment, as high environmental scores might indicate superior risk management in industries facing environmental regulation while being less relevant for service industries with minimal environmental impact. Companies in carbon-intensive industries might warrant higher valuations despite lower absolute environmental scores if they demonstrate superior environmental performance relative to industry peers or clear transition strategies toward more sustainable business models.

Social scoring examines factors including employee relations, customer satisfaction, community impact, product safety, and supply chain management that reflect companies' relationships with various stakeholders beyond shareholders. The measurement of social performance often proves more subjective than environmental metrics, as social impact can be difficult to quantify and may vary significantly across different cultural and economic contexts.

The relationship between social scores and financial performance often operates through indirect channels including employee productivity, customer loyalty, regulatory risk, and reputation effects that may not immediately appear in financial statements but can influence long-term competitive position and profitability. Companies with strong social performance might justify premium valuations due to reduced regulatory risk, superior employee retention, or stronger customer relationships that support sustainable competitive advantages.

Governance scoring evaluates board independence, executive compensation, shareholder rights, audit quality, and transparency that reflect the quality of corporate decision-making processes and alignment between management and shareholder interests. Governance factors often show the strongest correlation with financial performance among ESG categories, as good governance practices typically support better capital allocation decisions and reduce agency costs that can destroy shareholder value.

The interpretation of governance scores requires understanding that different governance structures might be appropriate for different companies based on their size, industry, ownership structure, and strategic situation. Family-controlled companies or founder-led businesses might show lower governance scores based on board independence metrics while actually demonstrating superior long-term decision-making that benefits shareholders through concentrated ownership and long-term strategic focus.

Greenwashing detection: Identifying genuine vs. marketing-driven ESG

Greenwashing represents one of the most significant challenges in ESG investing, as companies increasingly recognize the marketing and capital-raising advantages of appearing environmentally and socially responsible without making corresponding changes to their underlying business practices. Detecting greenwashing requires sophisticated analysis that goes beyond corporate sustainability reports and ESG scores to examine actual business practices, capital allocation decisions, and operational changes that indicate genuine commitment to ESG principles.

The most effective approaches to greenwashing detection focus on consistency between stated ESG commitments and actual business decisions, particularly regarding capital allocation, strategic planning, and operational changes that require significant resources and commitment. Companies engaging in genuine ESG improvements typically demonstrate this commitment through substantial capital investments, strategic business model changes, or operational modifications that involve meaningful costs and risks rather than simply improving disclosure or establishing sustainability committees.

Quantitative greenwashing detection often involves analyzing the relationship between ESG claims and measurable business metrics including capital expenditure patterns, revenue sources, regulatory compliance records, and third-party verification of sustainability claims. Companies making genuine ESG improvements typically show consistent patterns across multiple metrics rather than isolated improvements in easily manipulated disclosure measures.

The examination of executive compensation structures provides insights into whether ESG commitments represent genuine strategic priorities or superficial marketing efforts, as companies with authentic ESG focus typically incorporate sustainability metrics into executive compensation formulas while those engaged in greenwashing maintain traditional financial metrics without ESG components. The weighting and measurement of

ESG factors in compensation plans reveals the seriousness with which management approaches sustainability objectives.

Industry context becomes crucial for greenwashing detection, as ESG improvements that might be meaningful in one industry could represent minimal efforts in another context. Oil companies establishing renewable energy divisions might deserve credit for strategic diversification efforts, while technology companies making similar investments might simply be following industry trends without demonstrating meaningful ESG leadership relative to their industry peer group.

Third-party verification and certification provide additional validation for ESG claims, though the quality and independence of verification processes vary significantly across different certification systems. B-Corporation certification, carbon neutrality verification, and industry-specific sustainability certifications often provide more reliable validation than self-reported metrics or scores from rating agencies that primarily rely on corporate disclosures.

Impact measurement frameworks: Quantifying social and environmental returns

Impact measurement represents the systematic attempt to quantify the social and environmental outcomes generated by investments, going beyond traditional ESG analysis to measure actual positive impacts rather than simply avoiding negative outcomes. Effective impact measurement requires sophisticated frameworks that can attribute social and environmental changes to specific investments while accounting for additionality, time lags, and measurement uncertainty that characterize most impact outcomes.

The challenge of impact measurement stems from the difficulty of establishing causal relationships between investment activities and social or environmental outcomes that might be influenced by numerous other factors including government policy, technological change, and broader economic conditions. Successful impact measurement typically requires theory of change frameworks that explicitly model how investment activities are expected to generate specific outcomes through identifiable mechanisms that can be measured and validated over time.

Additionality analysis examines whether positive social and environmental outcomes would have occurred without the specific investment, addressing the fundamental question of whether impact investments actually create incremental positive change or simply redirect capital toward activities that would have happened anyway. This analysis requires understanding counterfactual scenarios and alternative funding sources that might have supported similar activities in the absence of impact-focused investment capital.

The time horizon for impact measurement often extends far beyond traditional investment evaluation periods, as many social and environmental changes require years or decades to fully manifest and measure accurately. Educational investments might require generational timeframes to demonstrate their full impact, while environmental restoration projects might need decades to show measurable ecosystem improvements that justify the original investment expenditures.

Social Return on Investment frameworks attempt to monetize social and environmental outcomes by assigning dollar values to benefits including reduced healthcare costs, improved educational outcomes, or environmental improvements that can be compared directly with financial returns to evaluate total return including both financial and social components. However, the monetization of social outcomes involves significant subjectivity and methodological challenges that can make SROI calculations misleading if not properly qualified and contextualized.

Standardization efforts including the Impact Management Project and Global Impact Investing Network have developed frameworks for impact measurement that enable comparison across different investments and sectors while maintaining flexibility for sector-specific metrics that reflect the unique characteristics of different types of impact investing. These standardization efforts help investors evaluate impact opportunities more systematically while avoiding the measurement inconsistencies that have historically plagued impact investing evaluation.

Conclusion: Your Investment Journey Forward

The journey from financial novice to sophisticated investor represents one of the most rewarding educational and wealth-building endeavors available to individuals willing to commit themselves to continuous learning and disciplined execution. Throughout this comprehensive exploration of investment principles, analytical frameworks, and practical strategies, we have constructed a foundation of knowledge that can support decades of successful investment decision-making. Yet understanding these concepts intellectually represents only the beginning of what must become a lifelong practice of applying, refining, and adapting these principles to changing market conditions and personal circumstances.

The transformation from passive observer of financial markets to active participant in wealth creation requires more than theoretical knowledge. It demands the development of emotional discipline, analytical skills, and strategic thinking that can only be cultivated through direct experience combined with systematic study and reflection. The investors who achieve superior long-term results typically distinguish themselves not through superior intelligence or access to exclusive information, but through their commitment to systematic approaches, continuous learning, and the emotional fortitude necessary to maintain perspective during the inevitable periods of uncertainty and volatility that characterize all financial markets.

Taking Your First Steps

The transition from investment theory to practice often represents the most challenging phase of the investor development process, as the security of academic understanding must give way to the uncertainty and responsibility of making actual financial commitments with real consequences. However, this transition need not be overwhelming when approached systematically with appropriate preparation, realistic expectations, and carefully managed risk exposure that enables learning without jeopardizing financial security.

Your 30-day action plan for getting started

The first thirty days of your investment journey should focus on establishing the foundational infrastructure and knowledge base necessary to support years of successful investing rather than rushing to make investment decisions that might prove premature or poorly informed. This initial period represents a crucial investment in your future success that can prevent many of the costly mistakes that derail investors who begin without adequate preparation.

Begin by conducting a comprehensive financial assessment that examines your current financial position, cash flow patterns, debt obligations, and insurance coverage to ensure that investing represents an appropriate use of available resources rather than a speculative distraction from more pressing financial priorities. Emergency fund establishment should precede investment activities for most individuals, as the psychological security of knowing that temporary setbacks cannot force premature investment liquidation provides the emotional foundation necessary for long-term investment success.

The establishment of clear financial goals provides the strategic context necessary for making informed investment decisions while maintaining focus during periods when market movements might otherwise encourage emotional decision-making. These goals should be specific, measurable, and time-bound while reflecting genuine priorities rather than vague aspirations that provide insufficient guidance for strategic decision-making. Writing down these goals and reviewing them regularly helps maintain strategic focus while providing benchmarks for measuring progress and adjusting strategies as circumstances change.

Education should consume a significant portion of these initial thirty days, with systematic study of investment fundamentals, market history, and analytical frameworks that provide the intellectual foundation necessary for informed decision-making. This educational process should combine theoretical study with practical application through simulated investment activities or paper trading that enables skill development without financial risk exposure.

Setting up your first brokerage account

The selection of a brokerage platform represents one of the most important infrastructure decisions in your investment journey, as this choice will influence your available investment options, transaction costs, research capabilities, and overall investment experience for years to come. The evaluation process should consider both current needs and anticipated future requirements, as switching brokerage platforms can be time-consuming and potentially costly once you have established positions and developed familiarity with specific systems.

Commission structures have become increasingly competitive across major brokerage platforms, with many offering commission-free stock and ETF trading that eliminates transaction costs as primary selection criteria. However, the absence of explicit commissions does not necessarily indicate the lowest total cost of ownership, as some platforms compensate for eliminated commissions through wider bid-ask spreads, payment for order flow arrangements, or other indirect costs that might exceed traditional commission structures for certain types of investors.

Research capabilities and educational resources provided by brokerage platforms can significantly enhance your investment analysis and decision-making capabilities, particularly during the early stages of your investment journey when comprehensive research access might justify higher costs or platform complexity. The quality and depth of fundamental analysis tools, technical analysis capabilities, and market commentary varies dramatically across different platforms, making it important to evaluate these resources relative to your analytical approach and learning objectives.

Account types and tax-advantaged options require careful consideration during the initial setup process, as decisions about traditional versus Roth IRA contributions, account titling, and beneficiary designations can have lasting implications for tax efficiency and estate planning objectives. Understanding the contribution limits, withdrawal rules, and tax implications of different account types helps optimize the tax efficiency of your investment strategy while ensuring compliance with regulatory requirements.

Technology platform usability becomes increasingly important as your investment activities expand and become more sophisticated, making it worthwhile to evaluate user interfaces, mobile capabilities, and customer support quality that will influence your ongoing investment experience. Some platforms excel at serving beginning investors with simplified interfaces and educational support, while others provide advanced capabilities that might be unnecessarily complex for investors in early stages of their development.

Making your first investment with confidence

The execution of your first investment represents a significant psychological milestone that transforms theoretical knowledge into practical experience while establishing the foundation for decades of wealth-building activities. This initial investment should be approached with careful preparation, realistic expectations, and position sizing that enables learning without creating undue financial or emotional stress that might undermine long-term investment discipline.

The selection of your first investment should prioritize learning opportunities and risk management over potential returns, as the educational value of this initial experience will influence your investment development far more than the specific financial outcomes. Broad-based index funds often provide ideal first investments because they offer immediate diversification, low costs, and performance benchmarks that enable evaluation of your investment progress relative to market averages without the complexity of individual stock analysis.

Position sizing for your first investment should reflect both your risk tolerance and learning objectives, with allocations large enough to create genuine engagement and attention but small enough that potential losses cannot materially impact your financial security or emotional well-being. Many experienced investors recommend starting with amounts that would be disappointing but not devastating to lose, enabling genuine market participation while maintaining perspective about the learning nature of these initial investments.

The timing of your first investment should balance preparation with action, avoiding both premature investments made without adequate knowledge and excessive delay caused by attempting to achieve perfect market timing or complete educational preparation. Market timing represents one of the most challenging aspects of investing even for experienced professionals, making it counterproductive to delay initial investments while waiting for ideal conditions that may never materialize.

Documentation and tracking systems should be established before making your first investment to ensure systematic monitoring of performance, dividends, and tax implications that will become increasingly complex as your portfolio grows. Simple spreadsheets or portfolio tracking applications can provide adequate initial infrastructure while enabling you to develop systematic approaches to performance measurement and tax record keeping that will serve you well throughout your investment journey.

Continuous Learning Path

Investment success requires a commitment to lifelong learning that extends far beyond initial education to encompass continuous adaptation to changing market conditions, evolving analytical techniques, and deepening understanding of economic principles that govern long-term wealth creation. The most successful investors typically distinguish themselves through their dedication to continuous improvement and intellectual curiosity rather than through innate intelligence or exclusive access to information.

Building your investment library

The development of a comprehensive investment library provides the intellectual foundation necessary for sophisticated investment analysis while serving as a reference resource for navigating challenging market conditions or evaluating new investment opportunities. This library should combine classic investment texts that provide timeless principles with contemporary works that address current market conditions and emerging analytical techniques.

The foundation of any investment library should include the works of Benjamin Graham, whose "The Intelligent Investor" and "Security Analysis" provide intellectual frameworks that remain relevant decades after their original publication. These texts establish principles of value investing, margin of safety, and rational analysis that serve as philosophical anchors during periods when market behavior might otherwise encourage emotional decision-making or speculative excess.

Warren Buffett's annual shareholder letters provide practical applications of investment principles through real-world examples and explanations of decision-making processes that illuminate how theoretical concepts translate into actual investment activities. These letters demonstrate long-term thinking, analytical rigor, and emotional discipline while providing insights into specific investment decisions and their rationales.

Contemporary investment literature should address current market conditions, technological developments, and analytical techniques that weren't available to earlier generations of investors while building upon timeless principles rather than contradicting them. Books addressing behavioral finance, quantitative analysis, and global investing provide modern perspectives that complement classic value investing approaches while addressing complexities of current market environments.

Industry publications and research reports from reputable investment firms provide ongoing insights into current market conditions, sector analysis, and economic trends that can inform investment decision-making while demonstrating professional analytical approaches. However, these sources should be evaluated critically for potential biases or conflicts of interest that might influence their recommendations or conclusions.

Finding mentors and communities

The development of mentoring relationships and participation in investment communities provides practical guidance, accountability, and support that can significantly accelerate learning while helping avoid common mistakes that often derail beginning investors. These relationships offer perspectives and experiences that cannot be gained through solitary study while providing encouragement during challenging periods when markets test investor resolve.

Professional mentoring relationships might develop through workplace connections, professional associations, or formal mentoring programs that match experienced investors with beginners seeking guidance. These relationships work best when based on mutual respect and clear expectations about time commitments, communication preferences, and areas where guidance is most valuable.

Investment clubs provide structured environments for learning about investment analysis while sharing research responsibilities and benefiting from diverse perspectives on investment opportunities. The most successful investment clubs focus primarily on education and analysis rather than performance competition, creating supportive environments where members can develop skills and confidence without pressure that might encourage poor decision-making.

Online communities and forums offer access to diverse perspectives and specialized knowledge while providing platforms for asking questions and sharing experiences with other investors. However, these communities require careful navigation to distinguish between valuable insights and misinformation while avoiding the groupthink that can undermine independent analysis and decision-making.

Professional conferences and educational seminars provide opportunities to learn from successful investors while staying current with market developments and analytical techniques. These events often provide networking opportunities and expose attendees to different investment approaches and perspectives that can broaden analytical frameworks and prevent intellectual stagnation.

Developing your unique investment edge

Long-term investment success often requires developing specialized knowledge, analytical approaches, or strategic advantages that enable you to identify opportunities or manage risks more effectively than the average market participant. This edge might stem from professional expertise, personal interests, analytical skills, or strategic approaches that align with your temperament and capabilities.

Professional or industry expertise can provide significant analytical advantages when applied to investment analysis of companies or sectors within your area of knowledge. Engineers might possess technical knowledge that enables superior evaluation of technology companies, while healthcare professionals might understand medical device or pharmaceutical companies better than generalist analysts who lack specialized training.

Geographic advantages might enable superior analysis of local or regional companies that receive limited attention from professional analysts based in major financial centers. Understanding local economic conditions, competitive dynamics, or management reputations can provide informational advantages that translate into superior investment performance when applied systematically.

Analytical approaches that suit your temperament and capabilities might provide sustainable competitive advantages when applied consistently over extended periods. Some investors excel at quantitative analysis and systematic approaches, while others possess superior qualitative judgment or behavioral analysis capabilities that enable them to identify opportunities that others miss.

Time horizon advantages might enable superior returns for investors who can maintain positions through complete market cycles while other participants face constraints that force short-term decision-making. Individual investors often possess natural advantages in this area compared to professional managers who face quarterly performance pressures or redemption risks that might force suboptimal timing decisions.

Long-Term Wealth Building

The ultimate objective of investment education and skill development should be the creation of sustainable wealth that can provide financial security, opportunity, and legacy for future generations. This wealth building process requires patience, discipline, and strategic thinking that extends beyond short-term market movements to focus on compound growth over multiple decades.

Milestone markers for your journey

Establishing clear milestones provides motivation and feedback that can help maintain focus during the extended time periods required for significant wealth accumulation while enabling periodic strategy adjustments based on progress and changing circumstances. These milestones should be meaningful yet achievable, providing genuine accomplishment while maintaining realistic expectations about wealth building timelines.

The first significant milestone often involves achieving positive net worth through debt reduction and initial investment accumulation, representing the transition from consumer to investor that establishes the foundation for future wealth building. This milestone requires discipline in spending, systematic saving, and initial investment success that demonstrates the viability of long-term wealth building strategies.

Portfolio diversification milestones might track progress toward optimal asset allocation across different asset classes, geographic regions, and investment strategies that reduce risk while maintaining growth potential. Achieving international diversification, alternative investment exposure, or sophisticated portfolio construction capabilities represents meaningful progress in investment sophistication and risk management.

Income replacement milestones measure progress toward financial independence by comparing investment income to living expenses, with various percentage targets representing increasing levels of financial security and flexibility. The achievement of ten percent, twenty-five percent, or fifty percent expense coverage through investment income provides concrete evidence of wealth building progress while establishing clear targets for future accumulation.

Absolute wealth targets should reflect personal financial objectives and lifestyle aspirations while accounting for inflation and changing circumstances that might affect future needs. These targets provide ultimate objectives for wealth building activities while enabling periodic reassessment of strategies and timeline expectations based on progress and changing market conditions.

Adjusting strategies as you grow

Investment strategies that prove effective during early wealth accumulation phases might require modification as portfolios grow in size and complexity while personal circumstances change through life stage transitions. Understanding when and how to adjust strategies helps optimize long-term wealth building while avoiding unnecessary changes that might disrupt successful approaches.

Asset allocation strategies typically require adjustment as portfolio values increase and risk tolerance evolves through different life stages. Younger investors might appropriately maintain higher risk portfolios focused on growth while older investors might gradually shift toward more conservative approaches that prioritize income and capital preservation.

Investment complexity can increase appropriately as knowledge and portfolio size grow, enabling access to alternative investments, individual security selection, or sophisticated strategies that might not be suitable or cost-effective for smaller portfolios. However, complexity should serve clear purposes rather than being pursued for its own sake, as simple approaches often prove more effective than elaborate strategies that exceed investor capabilities.

Tax optimization becomes increasingly important as portfolios and income levels grow, potentially justifying professional tax planning advice and more sophisticated strategies including tax-loss harvesting, asset location optimization, and estate planning considerations that weren't relevant during earlier wealth accumulation phases.

Geographic and currency diversification might become more important and feasible as portfolio size increases, enabling direct international investment or currency hedging strategies that provide risk management benefits while accessing global growth opportunities that domestic-only portfolios cannot capture.

Creating generational wealth

The transition from personal wealth accumulation to generational wealth creation requires strategic planning that extends beyond individual lifetimes to encompass family education, tax-efficient wealth transfer, and institutional structures that can preserve and grow wealth across multiple generations. This transition represents the ultimate evolution of investment strategy from personal financial security toward lasting family legacy.

Estate planning integration becomes crucial for substantial wealth preservation, requiring professional advice and sophisticated structures that can minimize estate taxes while ensuring smooth wealth transfer to intended beneficiaries. Understanding estate tax implications and available planning techniques helps optimize wealth transfer strategies while maintaining family control and values.

Family financial education represents one of the most important investments in generational wealth preservation, as subsequent generations must possess the knowledge and discipline necessary to preserve and grow inherited wealth rather than dissipating it through poor decision-making or lack of engagement. This education should begin early and continue throughout family members' development while emphasizing both technical knowledge and value systems that support responsible wealth stewardship.

Philanthropic strategies can provide tax benefits while creating family legacy and social impact that extends beyond pure wealth accumulation to encompass meaningful contribution to societal welfare. Charitable giving strategies including donor-advised funds, private foundations, or charitable trusts can provide tax-efficient methods for philanthropic activity while involving family members in meaningful social impact activities.

Your investment journey represents far more than a path to financial returns. It encompasses personal development, intellectual growth, and the acquisition of skills and perspectives that will serve you throughout your life while potentially benefiting future generations. The principles, strategies, and frameworks presented throughout this comprehensive guide provide the foundation for this journey, but your success will ultimately depend on your commitment to continuous learning, disciplined execution, and the patience necessary to allow compound growth to work its magic over the decades ahead.

The markets will test your resolve, challenge your assumptions, and occasionally humble your confidence. Economic cycles will create opportunities and risks that require adaptation while maintaining strategic focus. Technological developments will create new possibilities while potentially obsoleting established approaches. Through all these changes, the fundamental principles of rational analysis, emotional discipline, and long-term thinking will remain your most valuable tools for navigating uncertainty while building lasting wealth.

Begin today with confidence in your preparation, humility about the challenges ahead, and excitement about the wealth-building journey that awaits. The time spent mastering these concepts will pay dividends for the rest of your life, and the wealth you create will serve not only your own objectives but potentially provide opportunities and security for generations to come.

NOV 13 2025